Twayne's United States Authors Series

EDITOR OF THIS VOLUME

Kenneth Eble

University of Utah

Richard Palmer Blackmur

TUSAS 409

RICHARD PALMER BLACKMUR

By GERALD J. PANNICK

St. Mary's College

TWAYNE PUBLISHERS
A DIVISION OF G. K. HALL & CO., BOSTON

Copyright © 1981 by G. K. Hall & Co.

Published in 1981 by Twayne Publishers,
A Division of G. K. Hall & Co.
All Rights Reserved

Printed on permanent/durable acid-free paper and bound
in the United States of America

First Printing

Library of Congress Cataloging in Publication Data

Pannick, Gerald J
Richard Palmer Blackmur.

(Twayne's United States authors series ; 409)
Bibliography: p. 164–66
Includes index.
1. Blackmur, Richard P., 1904–1965—Criticism
and interpretation.   2.   Criticism—United States.
PS3503.L266Z83   801'.95'0924   80-27831
ISBN 0-8057-7338-X

To Henry Dan Piper

Contents

About the Author

The author holds degrees from the Universities of Connecticut and Southern Illinois and has taught Comparative Literature at St. Mary's College of Maryland for six years.

In addition to his teaching and writing, Dr. Pannick has served in the Maryland General Assembly and as Vice-Chairman of the Maryland Committee for the Humanities and Public Policy. He is currently a member of the Maryland Citizens Utility Board and is active in the business community.

Preface

The purpose of this first full-length study of Richard Palmer Blackmur's critical writings is to help explain some of the contradictory statements and ambiguous language in his essays; point out the continuity and changing emphases in his critical thinking; and contribute to a general reassessment of his place in the history of literary criticism.

My plan for the organization of this study was suggested by the nature of Blackmur's critical thought. In reading his essays, spanning some forty years, it became clear to me that Blackmur returned again and again to certain literary and critical problems. I have defined these problems in separate chapters and have grouped my consideration of relevant essays around them. Within each chapter my consideration of relevant essays dealing with each separate topic is arranged chronologically. I have not considered every essay that deals with each topic; rather, I have selected those essays I thought to be most representative of Blackmur's thinking.

This arrangement into separate chapters dealing with Blackmur's principal critical and literary concerns best untangles the strands of his thought. Even though my arrangement is not strictly chronological, I have attempted to give an indication of the changing emphases in his critical thinking. For instance, early in his career he was most interested in poetry and in its relationship to society. Therefore, after an introductory chapter, I first consider selected essays dealing with poetry. I turn next to Blackmur's interest in the role of the critic. I consider this topic second because it forms a bridge between the critical concerns of his early career to those of his middle career.

As Blackmur's career progressed, he became more and more interested in the social responsibilities of the critic. In developing this facet of his interest, Blackmur had a paradigm in Henry Adams. From the many essays dealing with the life and times of Henry Adams, I have selected for consideration those which most clearly present Blackmur's understanding of Henry Adams as a critic of culture.

In the following chapter I turn to a consideration of those essays that amplify another aspect of Blackmur's interest in the social responsibilities of the critic. In this chapter I have selected for critical attention essays that deal with what might be termed "moral action and personal fulfillment" in the European novel. Late in his career Blackmur focused his attention on such characters as Madame Bovary and Anna Karenina and wrote about them as if they were social critics whose commentary was embodied in their actions.

From there I go on to the critical concerns of Blackmur's last years. In this chapter I try to untangle the meaning of his later essays. I also try to explain why he wrote them in such an oracular style. I conclude my study with a consideration of Blackmur's contribution to literary criticism and his place in the history of criticism.

While Blackmur was best known as a critic, he was also a poet who published several volumes of poetry. The poetry is interesting and illustrative, not in the sense that it is a vade mecum to his criticism, but rather in that it indicates Blackmur's habit of mind in a more personal, less formal way than does the body of his criticism. For this reason I have considered his poetry in a chapter separate from his own criticism of poetry.

For various kinds of help I would like to thank the staffs of the Joseph Regenstein Library, University of Chicago, and the Department of Rare Books, Princeton University. For permission to quote from letters I would like to thank Richard Eberhart, Valerie Eliot, Allen Tate, the trustees of the Joseph Regenstein Library, University of Chicago, and the estate of Richard Palmer Blackmur. For permission to quote from Blackmur's published works I thank Harcourt, Brace, Jovanovich and Peter Smith, publishers. For permission to quote from material first presented by Blackmur at the Nagano, Japan Summer Seminar in American Literature in 1956, I thank the Kenkyusha Press, Tokyo.

Acknowledgements should also be given to Princeton University Press and the editors of *Hudson Review, Kenyon Review, Sewannee Review, Southern Review, Yale Review, Accent, Chimera,* and *The Virginia Quarterly Review.*

Preface

To my lovely wife Caroline Tedrow, I want to express my appreciation for her constant support and encouragement.

GERALD J. PANNICK

St. Mary's City, Maryland

Chronology

1904   Born January 21, Springfield, Massachusetts.

1922   Becomes a free-lance poet and critic in Cambridge, Massachusetts. "Discovers" Henry James.

1927   Begins association with *Hound and Horn.*

1928   Publishes two-part study of T. S. Eliot which establishes his reputation as a critic.

1930   Marries Helen Dickson.

1931   Leaves *Hound and Horn* editorship but continues to contribute critical essays.

1934   Publishes an essay on the *Prefaces* of Henry James in *Hound and Horn.*

1936   *The Double Agent,* first volume of collected criticism.

1937   Receives Guggenheim grant for study of Henry Adams. Publishes *From Jordan's Delight,* a volume of poetry.

1940   Becomes Allen Tate's assistant in Creative Writing Program at Princeton. Second collection of essays, *The Expense of Greatness* is published.

1942   *The Second World,* another volume of poetry.

1944   Spends year at the Institute for Advanced Study in Princeton.

1947   *The Good European and Other Poems.*

1948   Receives appointment in Department of English at Princeton.

1952   Promoted to full professor. Publishes two volumes of collected critical essays, *Language as Gesture* and *Form and Value in Modern Poetry.*

1955   *The Lion and the Honeycomb,* another volume of collected critical essays.

1956   Participates in the Nagano (Japan) Summer Seminar in American Literature. Gives four Library of Congress lectures which are published by the Library.

1959   *New Criticism in the United States,* a collection of critical essays.

1964   *Eleven Essays in the European Novel.*
1965   Dies February 2.
1967   A *Primer of Ignorance,* edited by Joseph Frank, is published.
1977   *Poems of R. P. Blackmur,* introduction by Denis Donoghue.
1980   *Henry Adams,* edited by Veronica Makowsky.

CHAPTER 1

Blackmur, New Criticism, and Blackmur's Critical Work

FOR most of his career, Richard Palmer Blackmur was well respected but little understood as a literary critic. Although not an officially recognized apologist for the New Criticism, he was early on associated with Allen Tate, John Crowe Ransom, Ivor Winters, Cleanth Brooks, and others who shared a concern for poetic language and technique and who ultimately established a body of literary criticism called the "New Criticism." Blackmur's assocation with this group, while based upon a number of common agreements concerning method and style, nevertheless led to misunderstandings and confused expectations regarding Blackmur's own critical writings. Blackmur was not a New Critic although many thought that he was. He had other literary concerns not shared by the New Critics and these other concerns ultimately became the focus of his criticism. He also developed a different style, unique to himself, with which to express his own ideas. However, the initial identification of Blackmur as a New Critic created, on the part of his readers, expectations concerning style and method which he invariably frustrated. The result was a general respect for his unusual literary intelligence coupled with a misapprehension of the purposes of his work.

The New Critics actually adopted Blackmur, who had, at the time, a more established critical reputation. In *The New Criticism* (1941), the book that gave the movement its name, John Crowe Ransom used several quotations from Blackmur's critical writings to define the New Criticism. Yet Ransom did not consider the theoretical underpinnings of Blackmur's criticism and, apart from a few references to Blackmur as a New Critic, mentioned only that his criticism was difficult rather than simple

15

and systematic. Blackmur did share with the New Critics an interest in the precise use of language in poetry and, also, an interest in establishing the legitimacy of poetry as a unique mode of apprehending and communicating reality. But Blackmur's interests in poetry extended also to the mind of the poet and to the place of the poet in society. These more Romantic interests were usually outside the scope of the New Critics' speculations. Blackmur, on the other hand, tended to emphasize precisely these interests, particularly so in the later stages of his career. But because he had been named a New Critic by Ransom, Blackmur was misunderstood when his essays treated subject matter supposedly outside the proper concerns of a New Critic.

Part of Blackmur's problem with being misunderstood was due to his style. His writing tended to be synoptic, oracular, and generally difficult to pin down to its precise meaning. A few critics of his work pointed out the apparent contradiction that Blackmur, who seemed to insist on precision and clarity in poetic language, could be so unclear and imprecise in his critical essays.

There was a reason for his opaque style. Blackmur believed that the modern critic had to build bridges between art and society in the twentieth century and that building these bridges necessitated an interpretative and creative approach to the practice of literary criticism. To Blackmur, social criticism could be based only upon an irrational, aesthetic experience of society and culture. But this experience had to be explained in rational terms. So, in effect, Blackmur was trying to write about an esthetic experience using the language of rational discourse. The effect on his style was predictable. It became increasingly "poetic" as he sought to describe his intuitive insights.

In the 1950s and 1960s, some of Blackmur's best critical essays were organic effusions tempered, he hoped, with poetic form to ensure that they would not be too idiosyncratic and undecipherable. In short, Blackmur adopted a style he thought best suited to the expression of interior states of mind. And because he adopted this kind of style to use in his critical essays, he frustrated and confused many who expected the clarity and precision of an objective analyst.

I Blackmur

When he died in 1965, Richard Palmer Blackmur had a distinguished reputation as one of America's leading literary critics. His reputation was based upon a prolific outpouring of essays that began in the 1930s and which continued unabated until his death. His initial success was a two-part study of T. S. Eliot's poetry that was published in the little magazine *Hound and Horn* in 1928. The essay on Eliot was followed by others on E. E. Cummings, W. B. Yeats, Wallace Stevens, Hart Crane, and Ezra Pound that firmly established his contemporary reputation.

An intensely private man, Blackmur maintained an impenetrable reserve toward those not his closest friends. A friend and colleague wrote that he was "a rather shadowy figure, and a lonely one. His students idolized him, yet always from a distance. Though he was patient and approachable, he paid them the ambiguous compliment of never condescending."[1] With friends, however, Blackmur could be affable and expansive. His knowledge was wide and he enjoyed extending it with good conversation over good food and drink.

Blackmur began his career in the 1920s as a free-lance poet and critic. By 1927, at the age of twenty-three, he had published poetry and critical reviews in the *Dial, Poetry Magazine,* and the *Saturday Review of Literature.* In that same year he began an association with a small literary magazine called *Hound and Horn,* edited by Lincoln Kirstein. It was as a major contributor and an associate editor of this magazine that Blackmur first made his name as a critic. He left the editorship in 1931 but continued to contribute critical essays and poems.

While he primarily wrote criticism and poetry during the 1930s, Blackmur also tried writing short stories, novels, and plays. Among his papers in the Blackmur Collection at Princeton University are some thirty-five short stories in various stages of completion, two unpublished novels, and two unproduced and unpublished plays. His poetry was more successful. Allen Tate said of Blackmur's first volume of poetry, *From Jordan's Delight,* that it was "the best American poetry of this decade."[2] His poetry, however, suffered from a lack of what Richard Eberhart called "the vital impulses."[3] And T. S. Eliot called his poetry "too thoughtful."[4] Others, and Blackmur himself, thought that he had too much of an analytical intelligence that tended to scatter his talent as a poet. His mind was subtle, flexible, with an extraordinary ability to synthesize his experience. But whatever the failings were in Blackmur's own poetry, his cool, lucid statements about poetic craft were helpful and encouraging to the generation of poets starting out in the 1930s and 1940s.

Blackmur was a poet who could write for other poets seriously interested in learning and mastering their art.

In 1937 Blackmur was awarded a Guggenheim grant to work on a critical interpretation of the life and work of Henry Adams. The significance of this project was that it opened up a whole new world of moral concerns that permanently affected his criticism. Like Adams, Blackmur began to see the artist as part of a vast social nexus with the primary responsibility of interpreting his society to his audience. After 1937, Blackmur's critical focus changed from the artwork to the artist as he began to concentrate on the function of the artist in mass society and on the role of the critic as intermediary between art and the public. These concerns took him out of the mainstream of critical activity in the 1940s and 1950s. On the strength of his earlier essays, however, his reputation continued to grow. In 1940 Blackmur became Allen Tate's assistant in the Creative Writing Program at Princeton and he stayed at Princeton in various capacities for the rest of his life. In 1952 he became a professor in the Department of English and initiated the Christian Gauss Seminars in criticism.

II   New Criticism

New Criticism developed in response to a new kind of poetry being written by T. S. Eliot, Ezra Pound, Wallace Stevens, W. B. Yeats, and others in the years following World War I. Essentially, their poetry used unfamiliar symbols and images as analogs of their feelings. Thus their poetry appeared to be more "private" than "public" and seemed to necessitate a critical methodology that could explain the unfamiliar symbols and images and which could elucidate what seemed to be a new and different sensibility.

The most important development in American letters during the 1930s and 1940s was the advent of the New Criticism. Its adherents, men like John Crowe Ransom, Cleanth Brooks, Ivor Winters, Allen Tate, I. A. Richards, and T. S. Eliot, focused their critical attention on the problem of establishing the legitimacy of poetry as a unique mode of apprehending reality and on the problem of establishing and defending an objective theory of value.

In attempting to establish the legitimacy of poetry as a unique mode of apprehending reality, the New Critics took into account the phenomenon of the poetic increment that seems to occur beyond what can be paraphrased about the poem after it is read. Ransom labeled the phenomenon "X." "The poem actually continues to contain its ostensible substance, which is not fatally diminished from its prose state: that is its logical core, or paraphrase. The rest of the poem is X, which we are to find."[5] Ransom and the others looked for the poetic increment in the structure of the poem.

In investigating structure the New Critics were trying to answer two interrelated questions: how could poetry be differentiated from other modes of apprehending and comprehending reality, and how could poetry have an unlimited range over human experience? To answer these questions the theory of contextualism was developed. Contextualism became an extremely complicated theory because each of the New Critics attempted to work out in a different way the difficulties encountered in trying to establish poetry as something unique. The theory behind contextualism centered upon the concept of the poetic context or framework. This framework consisted of words used in a certain way. Since both prose and poetry share a common language, the New Critics assumed that language works differently in poetry and that this difference makes poetry unique. They focused their attention on a characteristic of language that individual words can mean or refer to different things in different contexts. This referential characteristic of language did not itself differentiate poetry from prose, but it provided the basis for establishing poetry as a unique mode of discerning reality.

New Critical theorists decided that poetry was different from prose and therefore unique because poetry used language cross-referentially; that is, in their view, the words of a poem referred not to things in the outside world, but internally in the poetic context to the other words in the poem. The poem, then, was seen as a closed system. At the same time, however, the New Critics wanted the poem to express a wide range of human experience. This desire, however, was incompatible with poetry as a closed system of internally referential language. The words could not, at least theoretically, refer outside the poem to human experience. In other words, as a separate autonomous entity, the poem had no connection to anything else. If the New Critic held to his contextual differentiation between prose and poetry, he had to make clear just how the context managed to transform nonreferential language into universal expression. And this was difficult for him to do without vitiating the prose-poetry language difference. In fact, none of the New Critics was able, finally, to discover a theoretical justification that would allow the poem to be a closed system and yet refer to the world outside of itself.

In basing their distinction between prose and poetry on the referential characteristic of language, the New Critics combined two problems of language into one. They combined the problem of what words mean with the problem of their interrelationships. "First, there is the semantic problem, the problem of the denotative power of the word," Murray Krieger writes in his admirable study of New Critical theory.

Secondly, there is the structural problem, the problem of permissible relations among terms and propositions. The first is the problem of truth, of correspondence; the second the problem of validity, of coherence. If the second problem is subsumed by the first, as these critics indicate, then it is clear that the sole distinction between prose and poetry, may be found in the referential character of the former as against the self-contained, contextual character of the latter. But if the logical problem is properly seen as separate from the semantic problem, then indeed the foundations of the prose-poetry distinction based on referentiality, upon which modern criticism is built, are seriously shaken.[6]

In subsuming the logical (what words mean) aspect of language into the semantic (interrelationships between words) aspect of language, the New Critics were not only able to establish the uniqueness of poetry, they were also able to say that the logical aspect of language is controlled by the semantic aspect, or, in other words, the poetic context; or, form determines content. In practice, this meant that the New Critics paid most of their attention to the interrelationships between words in their poetry.

There was another theoretical difficulty involving the New Critics' desire for universality of poetic expression. The New Critics wanted for their subject matter an unlimited range of human experience. If this were allowed, then, any human experience could be the proper subject of poetry and anyone could write poetry. The New Critics were not about to be that democratic and they therefore developed a psychological description of the poetic process which established what "real" poets did when they created a poem. They introduced terms like *feeling, emotion,* and *sensibility* to describe what went on in the poet's mind. The distinctions among these terms were artificial and the whole description itself was somewhat mechanistic.

It was upon this psychological description of the poetic process and upon the structure of the poem that the New Critics based their declarations of value. What makes a good poem and how can a critic make anything other than a subjective judgment? These two questions are interrelated. The New Critics assumed that a poem has intrinsic value and that that value may be discovered by anyone. If the value or "goodness" of a poem is part of the poem itself and not dependent upon the subjective perception of an individual, then, they assumed, it was possible to determine the "objective" value of the poem. The New Critics determined value through their investigations of poetic structure. What makes a poem good, they said, can be determined through its structure because value is somehow "anchored" in the structure. In practice, the New Critics limited themselves to analyses of structure and made judgments of value only indirectly. That is, they decided what made a good poem and measured poetry by these criteria; yet they left the actual declaration of value unsaid. In later years Blackmur found this omission a great fault of the New Critics and consequently insisted that the critic must "come to judgment."

What, in the New Critic's view, were the structural aspects of a poem wherein resided poetic value and upon which they could at least theoretically make their judgments? These structural aspects proliferated as the New Criticism gained strength and stature in the American academy. The two most important were *irony* and *ambiguity.* These, of course, are functions of the way words interrelate in a specific poetic context. For the New Critic, they were aspects of language crucial to a good poem. Essentially, in practice, the New Critic decided value in poetry on the basis of how many different levels of meaning he could discover in the poem.

What was the function of the critic in New Criticism? What role did he play? Clearly, the demands made upon the critic in this theory were enormous. If value depended upon the levels of meaning in a poem, then the New Critical critic had to be able to master several disciplines and know something about various others. To be able to understand Eliot's *The Waste Land*, for instance, the New Critic needed to know prosody, psychology, history, anthropology, and some religion. In addition to the extraordinary demands made upon his knowledge, the New Critical critic needed to have a sensibility equal to that of the poet. Since his theory required him to make judgments in terms describing the poetic process he had to be able to recreate the poem in order to decide if the proper language had been used by the poet to express his feeling.

The theory behind the New Criticism may have lacked consistency at several points but it represented a point of view— an attitude—that enlivened a generation's appreciation of poetry and literature. "We developed a prodigious conscious skill in the psychology of poetic language," Blackmur wrote in 1951 looking backward to New Criticism's rise in the 1930s, "and entered thereby into the private worlds of the poets to find there private images of the great world not otherwise accessible to the reader and perhaps not otherwise creatable by the poet."[7] By the time the New Criticism became virtually the only critical method practiced in American universities in the 1950s, its practitioners had lost most of the elan and excitement of its originators. "So attractive as well as necessary were the techniques of this skill in language," Blackmur continued, "that they led to excess analysis, excess simplification, and excess application, which is the normal pathology of a skill become a method and a method become a methodology."[8]

Blackmur's own criticism exemplifies the best virtues of the New Criticism. Not a theorist himself, he was perhaps better able to avoid the doctrinal difficulties and consequently better able to apply the best insights of New Criticism. He insisted that poetry was a craft and that poetic language was unique and worthy of special attention. Sometimes pedantic in tone, his essays on particular poets gave, nonetheless, valuable insights into their work.

III   *Blackmur's Critical Work*

A topical arrangement divides Blackmur's critical work into four parts: criticism of poetry, criticism focused on the role of the critic, criticism of society and culture, and criticism devoted to the life and times of Henry Adams.

Most of Blackmur's criticism of poetry was written during the time of his association with *Hound and Horn*. The best essays were collected in *The Double Agent*, published in 1936. In these early efforts, Blackmur's critical focus was on language. He was interested in how words could be used to achieve certain poetic effects. In accordance with New Critical theory, his analyses of poetic language involved him in discussions of the poet's psychology. A typical Blackmurian judgment from this stage of his career is his finding in the work of E. E. Cummings a "sentimental denial of the intelligence . . . [that] appeals to the intellect which wishes to work swiftly and is in love with immediate certainty. A mind based on it accepts every fragment of experience as final and every notion as definite, yet never suffers from the delusion that it has learned anything."[9]

There were other critical interests in *The Double Agent* essays. Blackmur believed that interest in techniques had to extend also to "technique on the plane of intellectual and emotional patterns in Mr. [Kenneth] Burke's sense, in that there is a technique of securing and arranging and representing a fundamental view of life."[10] This is a typical Blackmurian interest which other New Critics did not develop but which is consistent with their critical orientation. If the critic is interested in the poet's mind because it affects his language and therefore the poem, then an analysis of the poet's mind apart from his poetry can be justified as a first step in understanding his poetry. The importance of this interest to Blackmur was such that early in his career he left the analysis of poetry to others and concentrated on the mind of the poet, then the minds of all artists, and finally on the minds of twentieth-century men.

Another interest prominent in *The Double Agent* essays was the role of the critic. Blackmur's description of the critic's job came to be the prototypical description of the New Critic. First the critic made an intensive study of the poem's language. When he had discovered as many levels of meaning as he could, using as much knowledge from various disciplines that he knew, the critic then made a leap of critical imagination and made a judgment. The critical act, Blackmur wrote,

consists first, in being willing to concentrate your maximum attention upon the work which the words and the motions of the words—and by motions I mean all the technical devices of literature—perform upon each other. Secondly, it consists in submitting, at least provisionally, to whatever authority your attention brings to light in the words. In doing this you will be following in pretty close parallel the procedure which the writer followed. Whether your submission is permanent or must be withdrawn will be determined by the judgment of all the standards and all the interest you can bring to bear. These will differ with the work at hand. But the act of submission must be made before you can tell; it is an act of imagination, not of will; and it is the enabling act of criticism.[11]

Blackmur extended the role of the critic beyond that of an assayer of value. In Blackmur's view, the interpretative function of the critic was supplemented by a social function. The social role of the critic, or "burden," as he termed it, was to be an intermediary between artists and their audiences. Blackmur believed that twentieth-century artists had lost their audiences and that their work was largely not understood. In an essay on James Joyce's *Ulysses* Blackmur wrote:

How .far has literature become inaccessible to its natural audience? How far has the natural audience (let us say for convenience the sum of those who go about the job of reading) itself lost the tools of access? Is it inevitable that the field of reference of the most responsible authors of our time should be largely unavailable to the most responsive existing audiences? Is it unavoidable that the area of conviction and belief that lies between such authors and such audiences should seem rather an area of the indifferent or the provisional? Is it necessary that the guidebook to the puzzle should replace the criticism of literature? How is it that the vice of scholarship should replace the elan of reading?[12]

To Blackmur, the critic became a secular priest. Not only did he interpret the sacred writ of modern literature to unwilling congregations, he also, by virtue of his criticism, gave direction and meaning to the lives of the artists and to those in the congregation. The critic gave faith and conviction.

In his later books, Blackmur further delineated the role of the critic and the place of literature in society. These concerns took him out of the mainstream of literary criticism, however, as those in the mainstream narrowed their critical foci and sharpened their technical skills in sterile analyses of language. Blackmur became something of an old-fashioned moralist in his concerns for the critic and for literature. Perhaps this is why the life of Henry Adams appealed to him.

Adams was nothing if not a moral man appalled by his century's cupidity and corruption. He was in Washington during Reconstruction and the Grant administration, and when he left government service he went on a spiritual quest seeking the conditions of spiritual fulfillment. To Blackmur, Adams was the supreme critic because he tried to interpret his times and give faith and direction to himself and to his generation. Blackmur's first essay on Henry Adams was published in 1940 in a collection of essays entitled *The Expense of Greatness.* Several other essays on Adams appeared but Blackmur's projected critical biography was never finished. (The manuscript has been edited and published.) His interest in Adams and the thrust of the essays in this volume developed themes and concerns present in *The Double Agent* yet marked a turning away from specifically literary concerns to those that might be termed literature-in-society. The volumes of collected essays published after 1940 restated in ever-subtler formulations Blackmur's concern for the place of literature in society.

Blackmur's Library of Congress lectures, given in 1956 and posthumously published in 1967, deserve special note for their style. Entitled *Anni Mirabiles 1921-1925: Reason in the Madness of Letters,* they covered various symptoms and aspects of modern culture. They were written in an oracular, intimating, puzzling, and poetic style that made them prose poems. Their importance in Blackmur's work lies in the fact that they are his attempt at criticism as a work of art. Blackmur meant these essays to express the cultural situation—not directly, as any traditional critical essay might—but indirectly and dramatically, as a novel or poem would.

IV   *Influences on Blackmur*

There were two people who had a seminal and lasting effect on Blackmur's work as a critic. The first is T. S. Eliot, who influenced Blackmur's thinking on the poetic process, and the second is Henry James, whose life in art provided Blackmur his critical sensibility. In 1928 Blackmur wrote a two-part study of Eliot's poetry for *Hound and Horn* in which he described Eliot's conception of the poetic process. In the years following, Blackmur's own criticism of poetry bore Eliot's influence. The poetry essays collected in *The Double Agent* are practical applications of Eliot's ideas, but Blackmur did not imitate Eliot's criticism; rather, he adopted a description of the creative process that he found workable and useful. Through Eliot, Blackmur found himself in the intellectual company of Wordsworth and Coleridge insofar as New Criticism is an extension of Romantic critical theory with its interest in the psychology of the poet and organic form.

The second major influence on Blackmur was Henry James. In an essay on James's *Prefaces* written in 1934, again for *Hound and Horn*, Blackmur wrote that James

wanted the truth about the important aspects of life as it was experienced, and he wanted to represent that truth with the greatest possible lucidity, beauty, and fineness, not abstractly or in mere statement, but vividly, imposing on it the form of the imagination, the acutest relevant sensibility, which felt it. Life itself—the subject of art—was formless and likely to be a waste, with its situations leading to bewilderment; while art, the imaginative representation of life, selected, formed, made lucid and intelligent, gave value and meaning to, the contrasts and oppositions and processions of the society that confronted the artist.[13]

These artistic goals and the sensibility that made their achievement possible became Blackmur's critical goals. To Blackmur, criticism also created, formed, and made lucid and meaningful the life he lived.

CHAPTER 2

Blackmur on Poetry

I have divided this chapter into two major parts. In the first part I will try to present as clearly as possible Blackmur's thoughts on the poetic process. In the second part I will review six representative essays on various poets in which his views on poetry are put into practice. Nowhere in Blackmur's own work or in essays about his work is there a discussion devoted solely to the theory underlying his critical assessments. Setting forth his theory and following that exposition with examples of his critical practice should lead to a larger understanding of Blackmur's function as a critic.

I Theory

In the interests of clarity, I have divided my discussion of Blackmur's poetic theory into subsections on the poet, the poem, and the reader.

A. The Poet

To Blackmur, the writing of poetry involved a psychological process which he explained in terms of how he understood the poet's mind worked. Before explaining that process, the very first question to be asked is how does Blackmur differentiate between the poet and the nonpoet? He answers by stating that the poet has a "talent for significant experience."[1] Any artist's native talent, Blackmur says, "will be for perceiving apples, and anything else, in this way: they should be directly felt, perceived not as free sensation, which is impossible, nor with an idea of action, which is irrelevant, but for the sake of its being and meaning."[2] The poet is different from the nonpoet, then, in that he "feels" more directly and observes experience for its own

27

sake. The importance of this distinction is that, in claiming the poet has a somewhat different relationship to his experience than does the nonpoet, Blackmur can then analyze the poet's mind for the source of this difference, after which he can then discuss how this difference affects the medium of language and turns it into poetry.

Blackmur's description of the poetic process begins with a division of the mind into two parts—reason and imagination. The function of the poet's reason is "the recognition and creation of order where disorder was."[3] The function of the poet's imagination is to make the mind's "discourse (or concourse) in images and idioms as meaningful as the original parallel experiences seemed when experienced in life."[4] These two terms are defined in this way because Blackmur believes that poetry begins in the poet's consciousness or "feeling states" wherein the flux of images and feelings have no order other than a sequential order; and, later, when these images and feelings must be recalled, the poet's imagination must make them "as meaningful as the original parallel experiences seemed when experienced in life." "The flux of images in the consciousness," Blackmur writes, "may be said to move logically, in that one feeling state produces another; a process of which the best evidence is in ordinary daydreaming. The use of the word logical is thereby possible because the connections between a sequence of images are, so far as we can observe, like those implied in a sequence of numbers; where the sequence 1, 2, 3, . . . implies infinity."[5] The poet perceives his reality as a flux of images and his reason and his imagination work upon those images to produce the poem. But how?

Art, Blackmur says, involves a transmutation of ordinary "experience into so precise a form that it cannot be redefined qualitatively, and must be understood as the expression of sensibility."[6] The imagination is the catalyst in the transmutation process. It seizes "the individual from the flux and any qualification, any evaluation, whether in morals or art, is imaginative."[7] The imagination qualifies, evaluates, and reintensifies the particular experience or set of experiences the poet is recalling for poetic purposes. But experience acted upon by the imagination must be patterned, controlled, and ordered. This is reason's function. In other words, reason recalls past experience (and is equated with memory) and makes that experience intelligible in terms other people may understand.

In his essay on E. E. Cummings, Blackmur wrote that "unintelligibility is a necessary consequence of such a pursuit [Cummings's desire to deny reason in his poetry] if by the intelligible we mean something concrete, qualified, permanent, and public. Poetry, if we understand it, is not in immediacy at all. It is not given to the senses or to the free intuition."[8] The key terms are "concrete" and "public" because, for reason to make the poet's experience intelligible, the experience must be organized into a form which is its concrete, public manifestation. "The chaos of private experience," Blackmur stated, "cannot be known or understood until it is projected and ordered in a form external to the consciousness that entertained it in flux."[9] To understand the meaning of the term "form" as it is used here, I must first introduce three terms from Blackmur's essay "In the Hope of Straightening Things Out."[10] These terms are "feeling," "emotion," and "sensibility." They are Eliot's terms and they are taken from an essay in which Blackmur is describing Eliot's notions of the creative process. They are applicable, however, to a reconstruction of Blackmur's poetic theory since his practical criticism shows evidence of their presence.

As the series of images flows into the poet's consciousness, his sense of their presence Blackmur calls feeling. "Feeling is the fundamental term; concrete, sensory, nuclear, somehow in experience, whether actual or imagined." The poet's emotions are "feelings, organized, generalized, abstracted, built into a form, theoretic or not." The poet's sensibility is "his stock, his reservoir, his cumulus of feelings and perceptions in various states of organization; and thus represents his residual skill to respond sensibily. Sensibility is what you draw on to make fresh responses. Live language and particularly live poetry make the great objective reservoir of sensibility; the traditional and impersonal source of what power you have over your own sensibility." It is now possible to describe what Blackmur means by "form." The poet's sense that something is happening to him, that he is having a significant or poetic experience, is categorized as a feeling. When the poet has a feeling, he does not know what he feels, only that he senses something. At this point, according to Blackmur, the poet's reason puts a name to what he feels and

the feeling immediately becomes an emotion. To put a name to a
feeling involves memory, of course, and Blackmur has called
reason "the living memory of the mind" in his essay "The Great
Grasp of Unreason." Blackmur calls emotion the form of feeling
and distinguishes between feeling and emotion by using the
following paradigm: "You can hurt a man's feelings, you cannot
hurt a man's rage; but you can rouse his rage by hurting his
feelings." This distinction is important in Blackmur's canon
because, as we shall see, his criticism of the poetry of both
Cummings and D. H. Lawrence is that they try to express their
feelings directly in their poetry without first using their reason to
establish forms for them—that is, establish the feelings as
emotions. It is Blackmur's contention that the poet never directly
expresses his feelings. "Properly speaking a poet, or any man,
cannot be adequate to himself in terms of himself. True
consciousness and true expression of consciousness must be
external to the blind seat of consciousness—man as sensorium.
Even a simple image must be fitted among other images, and
conned with them, before it is understood. That is, it must take a
form in language which is highly traditional and conventional."[11]
To use Blackmur's example, the poet as sensorium feels
something which his reason tells him is rage. Rage is not the
feeling but the emotion, and, as such, is the form which the
feeling takes.

   With this distinction between feeling and emotion in mind, we
can go on to a consideration of the remaining two elements of the
poet's mind—his imagination and his sensibility. As Blackmur
sees it, the function of the imagination is to make the mind's
"discourse (or concourse) in images and idioms as meaningful as
the original parallel experiences seemed when experienced in
life." When the poet wants to recall a certain poetic experience,
his reason recalls it for him. What is actually recalled is the
emotion, not the *actual* experience which would be his feeling.
There is a loss of intensity from the time a poet has a feeling to
the time that feeling becomes an emotion, so that the job of the
imagination is to give to the emotion approximately the same
intensity as the original feeling. "Emotions in art," Blackmur
says, "are never reproductions of experience, but its result."[12] As
a *result* of the poet's experience, emotions do not have the
intensity of experience, but, he says, "a dog's dying howl [a
recalled emotion or experience of the poet] may be made to

express in itself the whole tragedy of life, which it indeed may or may not do, depending on the reach of the imagination, or represented experience, you bring to bear on it."[13]

The reach of the poet's imagination, his ability to give to emotions the intensity of feelings, is a function of his sensibility which is his "residual skill to respond." Sensibility is the poet's capacity to respond or have significant experiences and, in Blackmur's view, is the poet. "A change in sensibility is equivalent to a change in identity, a change in soul. Sensibility is the faculty, the working habit of the intelligence; and as such is the stress and habit of experience."[14] A unified sensibility is crucial to successful poetry and can be achieved, Blackmur says, if the poet has an all-embracing attitude toward life. "The necessity for great art is the necessity of completeness, the necessity of a complete attitude towards life. A philosophy is not necessary—as in Shakespeare, or if present is not used as a philosophy—as in Dante. But a view of life cannot be absent."[15] Blackmur's theoretical treatment of poetic creativity is controlled by the concept of sensibility. Unity or completeness of the sensibility means having an integrated mind where reason and imagination are balanced. And when this integrated mind sets to work in language, great poetry is the result.

B. *The Poem*

In Blackmur's poetic theory, the poem is not a self-contained autonomous entity but, rather, the link between poet and reader. The most important element in the poem is language, and this is the element upon which Blackmur focuses much of his critical attention. The one great principle of poetic language, Blackmur says, is "the principle that the reality of language, which is a formal medium of knowledge, is superior and anterior to the reality of the uses to which it is put."[16] To explain, Blackmur notes that

when a word is used in a poem it should be the sum of all its appropriate history made concrete and particular in the individual context; and in poetry all words act *as if* they were so used, because the only kind of meaning poetry can have requires that all its words resume their full life: the full life being modified and made unique by the *qualifications* the words perform one upon the other in the poem. Thus even a very bad poem may seem good to its author, when the author is not an acute critic and believes that there is life in his words merely because there was life (and a very different sort of life, truly) in the feelings which they represent. An author should remember, with the Indians, that the reality of a word is anterior to, and greater than, his use of it can ever be; that there is a perfection to the feelings in words to which his mind cannot hope to attain, but that his chief labour will be toward the approximation of that perfection.[17]

There are three ideas in these two statements about language which deserve emphasis. The first is that words have a life of their own and are "superior and anterior to the reality of the uses to which" they are put. Blackmur means, quite literally, that words have a history in the Oxford English Dictionary that cannot be ignored by the poet and must be taken into account. For example, Cummings used the word "flower" "as a maid of all work . . . and in the process has deprived the word of its history, its qualities, and its meaning."[18] When words are deprived of their histories, qualities, and meanings, the poem becomes "permanently abstract and unknowable for the reader, and remains altogether without qualifications and concreteness."[19] The words of the poem present only an impenetrable surface.

The second idea is that the words in the poem are "modified and made unique by the *qualifications* the words perform one upon the other in the poem." That is, the meaning of individual words in a poem are modified by their context. "Any use of a word stretches it slightly, because any use selects from among many meanings the right one, and then modifies that in context."[20] Blackmur's criticism of the phrase "funest philosophers" in Wallace Stevens's poem "Of the Manner of Addressing Clouds" might be helpful in illustrating this point. Within the context of Stevens's poem, Blackmur says, "the word funest is not so much itself stretched by its association with philosophers as the word philosophers—a common word with many senses— stretches funest. That is, because Mr. Stevens has used the word funest, it cannot easily be detached and used by others. The point is subtle. The meaning so doubles upon itself that it can be understood only in context. It is the context that is stretched by the insertion of the word funest; and it is that stretch, by its ambiguity, that adds to our knowledge."[21] The meanings of individual words are not only modified by their context, they are also subordinated to the total meaning of their context. The meanings of words in a poem may only be understood in context. "That is one business of poetry, to use words to give quality and feeling to the precious abstract notions, and so doing to put them beyond words and beyond the sense of words."[22] The total meaning of a poem will be more than the sum of the meanings of its individual words.

The third idea in Blackmur's thought on poetic language is "that there is a perfection to the feelings in words to which [the poet's] mind cannot hope to attain; but that his chief labour will be toward the approximation of that perfection." Blackmur means that the poet must wrestle with his medium and that the words he chooses will only approximate his feelings. In Blackmur's theory, words can only approximate feelings because they are forms or conventions in language. The poet, Blackmur says, never expresses himself directly; that is, the poet never expresses his feelings, only his emotions which are forms of the feelings. Emotions are expressed in language by terms like "rage." The difference between the form of a feeling which is characterized with a generic term like "rage" and the actual private experience of the poet is that there is a loss in intensity— language reduces the intensity of the feeling; and, further, most words used to signify feelings are "highly traditional and conventional."[23] Blackmur means words like "love," "spring-time," and any other hackneyed term which has become useless to express any private intensity at all because of its long use. "Words long used lose their original shape and accrue to themselves much irrelevant colour and connotation:—so when the outline is obliterated, the meaning also passes or loses altogether its denoting limits."[24]

The relationship of the poem to the poet is that the poem is the expression of the poet's experience. In his essay on Cummings, Blackmur mentions that he regards poetry as "expression, as statement, as presentation of experience." Since expression depends upon language, the binding tie between poet and poem must be the words the poet uses to write his poem. In poetry, Blackmur says, the language must be in proportion to "the feelings which it denotes."[25] In order for language to be in proportion to his feelings, the poet must have "a fresh feeling for language—a feeling at once for the precision and indefinable suggestive qualities of words as they take hold of and signify things."[26] What does Blackmur mean by proportion in poetry? Again in the Cummings essay, he writes, "True meaning (which is here to say knowledge) can only exist where some contact, however remote, is preserved between the language, forms, or symbols in which it is given and something concrete, individual, or sensual which inspired it; and the degree in which the meaning is seized will depend on the degree in which the particular concreteness is realized." Meaning depends upon the contact between the words of the poem and the feelings which inspire those words. Proportion in poetry is this contact between feelings and words. The words a poet uses should indicate his feelings. An example from Blackmur's criticism of Cummings will illustrate proportion.

In Cummings's *Tulips and Chimneys,* "there is a poem whose first and last lines supply an excellent opposition of proper and improper distortion of language." The first line is "the Cambridge ladies who live in furnished souls"; the last line is "the moon rattles like a fragment of angry candy." "In the context," Blackmur continues,

the word "soul" has the element of surprise which is surprise at *justness;* at *aptness;* it fits in and finishes off the notion of the line. "Furnished souls" is a good, if slight, conceit; and there is no trouble for the reader who wishes to know what the line means; he has merely to *extend* his knowledge slightly, just as Mr. Cummings merely extended the sense of his language slightly by releasing his particular words in this particular order. The whole work that the poet here demands of his reader is pretty well defined. The reader does not have to *guess;* he is enabled to *know.* The reader is not collecting data, he is aware of a meaning.

In Blackmur's judgment, the poet's feelings are in proportion to the words in the first line. In the second line, however,

We can say that Mr. Cummings is putting beauty next to the tawdry; juxtaposing the dead with the live; or that he is being sentimentally philosophical in verse—that is, releasing from inadequate sources something intended to be an emotion. As the most common form of sentimentality is the use of emotion in *excess* of its impetus in the feelings, here we have an example of emotion which fails by a great deal to *come up* to its impetus. It is a very different thing from understatement, where the implications are always definite and where successful disarming.

In other words, the words in this second line do not match or indicate what Blackmur assumes to have been the strong feeling behind them. This is an example of a lack of proportion in poetic language.

C. *The Reader*

The relationship of the poem to the reader is that the poem is a source of knowledge for the reader. "The question is," Blackmur says, "not what one shares with the poet, but what one knows in the poem." This is an important point. Blackmur does not think of the poem as a medium of communication between the poet and the reader. "It should be confessed," he says,

> that for all those persons who regard poetry only as a medium of communication, these remarks are quite vitiated. What is communicated had best remain as abstract as possible, dealing with the concrete as typical only; then "meaning" will be found to reside most clearly in the realm of ideas, and everything will be given as of equal import. But here poetry is regarded not at all as communication but as expression, as statement, as presentation of experience, and the emphasis will be on what is made known concretely.[27]

Of the reader Blackmur says:

> So far as he is able, the reader struggles to reach the concrete, the solid, the definite; he must have these qualities, or their counterparts among the realm of the spirit, before he can understand what he reads. To translate such qualities from the realm of his private experience to the conventional forms of poetry is the problem of the poet; and the problem of the reader, likewise, is to come well-equipped with the talent and the taste for discerning the meaning of those conventions as they particularly occur. Neither the poet's casual language nor the reader's casual interlocution is likely to be much help. There must be a ground common but exterior to each: that is the poem.[28]

The poem, then, is not a medium of communication but the common ground between the poet and reader. The reader must bring to the poem as "much talent and taste for discerning the meaning" of the poem as he can. The poet must write the poem so that it is capable of being deciphered. The knowledge the reader gains is knowledge of the poet's experience. And this knowledge is gained through his, the reader's, aesthetic experience of the poem. Blackmur is less clear on this point than on any of the other points under discussion, but I think that an illustrative example from his essay on Wallace Stevens will illuminate what he means by the aesthetic experience.

In reviewing Stevens's "Sea Surface Full of Clouds" Blackmur says, "Neither the material of the poem nor what we get out of it is by nature susceptible of direct treatment in words." Blackmur would say this about all poetry; what we derive from it—our aesthetic experience of it—is by its nature not susceptible to treatment in words. We cannot exactly say what it is but we can say what the aesthetic experience involves.

The general position of a critic, or of any mind aware of its responsibilities, is liable to change when the impetus of thought is altered in mode or intensity; but the change, in an interested mind, will usually occur along a line the chart of which only ignorance prevents us from predicting. The past will not be destroyed nor its sense often confuted; but understood with a different emphasis, reproportioned by the present interest so as to maintain its usefulness. If the change turns out well we call it growth, and say it represents an increase in the depths of personality, the dimensions of sensibility.[29]

In short, the aesthetic experience of a poem involves a change in the reader's sensibility.

There are a few more general comments about Blackmur's poetics that might be made before going on to the second part of this chapter. Let me say again that the foregoing was a hypothetical formulation derived from among the critical judgments made in his essays. There are inconsistencies and ambiguities which Blackmur would have paid more attention to if he had been interested in developing a systematic poetics; but, allowing for that there are several things that might be pointed out.

The description of the poetic process is a very mechanistic one. In creating the poem the poet seems to do no more than to find verbal forms for his feeling-states; and these verbal forms must be in proportion to those states. Poetic creativity, in Blackmur's description, involves a simple translation of a sensuous image fluxing across the consciousness into an understandable form, and this makes the poet simply the agent of translation. The incalculable human element is reduced here to a calculable, conscious activity of finding verbal correlatives for feeling-states. The criterion of proportion further establishes the mechanistic nature of the poetic process. If the poet is to use words in proportion to his feelings, then he must understand his own feelings before he finds verbal forms for them. How else would he be able to know whether the words were in proportion to his feelings? If the poet already understands his feelings, then finding verbal correlatives does not even help him psychologically and further reduces what he does to a mechanical activity. It is interesting to note that Blackmur values those poets who seem to be the most conscious craftsmen of poetry and dislikes those whose poetry seems to be spontaneous and emotional.

The problem with a mechanistic concept of the poetic process is that it undercuts the uniqueness of poetry and the poet. Theoretically anyone can do or be taught to do what the poet does; and, upon further reflection, it may be remarked that finding verbal correlatives for feeling-states is what everyone does anyway. How then would Blackmur, with his mechanical concept of the creative process, reestablish the uniqueness of poetry and the poet? In terms of Blackmur's theory enumerated above, poetry is unique because of the way its medium is "modified and made unique by the qualifications the words perform one upon the other in the poem." These qualifications seem to be the interconnecting levels of meaning the words establish in the poem. So the uniqueness of poetry is once again reestablished without contradicting the mechanical nature of its manufacture. In fact, because of the many meanings a word, and many words taken together, can have, any one poet or critic cannot, Blackmur has said, take them all into consideration. The poem, in his view, therefore becomes more than just a product manufactured by the poet—it takes on a life of its own. The uniqueness of the poet lies in his all-embracing sensibility. His ability to unite disparate experience is due to the balance in his mind of reason and imagination; that is, the two modes of mind which make his experience intelligible and vital.

Critical judgments in Blackmur's scheme are based upon the poet's manipulation of his medium and upon the critic's perception of the poet's sensibility as evidenced in his poetry. A good poem shows evidence that the poet was aware of a large number of the interconnecting meanings his choice of words produced. To judge this, the critic tries to recreate in the critical act what the poet went through in the creative act. He is then able to tell whether the poet's words were in proportion to his feelings because he has experienced the same feelings. A good poet is one who can make his experience intelligible because he has a unified sensibility. By now it must be obvious that Blackmur's critical judgments in the following section will be far from "objective." In historical terms, Blackmur's judgments on poetry are based upon an expressive theory of poetic creation that is very close to Coleridge's yet which at the same time puts a great deal of emphasis upon the classicist's concern for the medium.

II Practice

Blackmur's essays on E. E. Cummings, Hart Crane, D. H. Lawrence, Wallace Stevens, W. B. Yeats, and T. S. Eliot serve especially to illustrate how his thoughts on poetic expression are manifested in his criticism of their poetry. According to Blackmur, the basic fault of the first three named is that their poetry making is too spontaneous, too much without the intellectualizing power of the reason. The last three named fulfill the requirement of a unified sensibility that is necessary for great poetry.

A. E. E. Cummings

"The poet," Blackmur begins, "does not ever express himself privately. The mind cannot understand, cannot properly know its owns musings until those musings take some sort of conventional form." Blackmur means that the only way the poet's felt experience can be made intelligible, even to himself, is through the workings of reason and imagination in finding a conventional form for that felt experience. Felt experience or feeling is a unique and private sensation until reason and imagination make it intelligible and communicable. In Blackmur's view, Cummings's mistake in his writing is double in assuming first that feelings are intelligible in the mind before reason and imagination come into play; and second, that the poet can directly transfer feelings to a poem without using conventions and yet render those same feelings intelligible to his readers. Cummings believes, Blackmur states, that "a poem, because it happens, must mean something and mean it without relation to anything but the private experience which inspired it. Certainly it means something," Blackmur continues, "but not a poem; it means that something exciting happened to the writer and that a mystery is happening to the reader." But even this kind of ambiguous meaning is conveyed, however inadequately, through the conventions of language. Poets like Cummings "do not write without conventions, but being ignorant of what they use, they resort most commonly to their own inefficient or superficial conventions [and] the effect is convention without substance; the unique experience becomes a rhetorical assurance." In other words, Cummings's conventions do not adequately convey his experience. And because the language conventions he does choose are, in Blackmur's opinion, "inefficient" and "superficial" they do not convey his meaning to his readers. The reader creates something of his own. For instance, the line "the moon rattles like a fragment of angry candy" in Cummings's poem "Sonnets-Realities I" is difficult to understand because "in the process of understanding the meaning of the words themselves disappears. The thrill of the association of 'rattles' with 'moon' and 'angry' with 'candy' becomes useless as a guide. . . . It leaves the reader at a loss; where it is impossible to *know*, after any amount of effort and good will, what the words mean." Cummings's inability to convey meaning adequately, Blackmur continues, is due directly to his careless attitude toward language; that is, his careless attitude toward what words mean. The way Cummings uses words wipes "out altogether the history of the word, its past associations, and general character." The reader can only understand Cummings by intuition because the "the reality, the event, the feeling, which we will allow Mr. Cummings has in mind, is not sensibly in the word."

Cummings's poetry produces, Blackmur says, not meaning but thrill. To illustrate, Blackmur uses Cummings's phrase "scythe takes crisply the whim of thy smoothness." He objects to the way "crisply," "whim," and "smoothness" interact with each other to destroy any possible meaning. The scythe (which Blackmur thinks may be the scythe of death) is combined with "three unusually sensed words for the sake of the *thrill* the special combination might afford." Blackmur continues: "As the phrase

stands there is no precision in it. There is a great suggestion of
precision about it—like men going off to war; but precisely *what*
is left for the reader to guess, to supply from his own heart."
Blackmur concludes that "the three words are unalterably
combined by the force of *crisply* in such a way as to defeat the
only possible sense their *thrilling* use would have had." Blackmur
suggests that poets like Cummings who use tactile and visual
images should "escape the prison of their private minds; to use in
their poems as little as possible of the experience that happened
to them personally, and on the other hand to employ as much as
possible of that experience as it is data." The poet should submit
his feelings to his reason and imagination. Reason will find
intelligible forms for the feelings and imagination will give life
and vitality to those forms. Poetry, in Blackmur's opinion, is not
immediate experience but experience after it has been worked
on by reason and imagination. This is an interesting parallel to
William Wordsworth's definition of poetry as "the spontaneous
overflow of powerful feelings" recollected in tranquillity.
Blackmur would stress the "recollected in tranquillity." "Poetry," he continues, "if we understand it at all, is not in immediacy
at all. It is not given to the senses or to the free intuitions."
Cummings's poetry and the poetry of other "sentimental and
romantic writers" will always have a freshness and "ominous
glow of immediacy"; but their poetry will only be understood by
accident—insofar as the sensation felt by the poet and communi-
cated to the poem, however inadequately, matches a similar
sensation in the reader.

To Blackmur the function of poetry is to communicate
meaning in the hope of establishing in the reader an experience
identical to that felt by the poet. What irritates Blackmur most
about Cummings and poets like him is that they think they are
communicating meaning. "But no poetry is so pretentious,"
Blackmur says. "No poetry ever claimed to mean more; and in
making this claim it cannot avoid submitting itself, disastrously,
to the criticism of the intelligence. So soon as we take it seriously,
trying to discover what it really says about human destiny and
the terms of love and death, we see how little material there is in
this poetry except the assurance, made with continuous gusto,
that the material exists." In summary, Blackmur's quarrel with
Cummings is with his "sentimental denial of the intelligence and
the deliberate assertion that the unintelligible is the only object

of significant experience." Cummings's denial of the intelligence (or the ordering function of his reason) is a result of his assumption that "because experience is fragmentary as it strikes the consciousness it is thought to be essentially discontinuous and therefore essentially unintelligible except in the fragmentary form in which it occurred." In Blackmur's view, this assumption leads to the double fallacy of believing "in the inexorable significance of the unique experience" and discarding as a consequence of that belief "the only method of making the unique experience into a poem—the conventions of the intelligence."

B. D. H. Lawrence

Blackmur's criticism of Lawrence's poetry is essentially the same as his criticism of Cummings's poetry. Both lack evidence of reason in their poetry because both try to put their feelings directly into their work. The evidence lies in their poetic language. Neither, Blackmur thinks, has the sensitivity for language that is required to write great poetry. The difference between the two is that where Cummings was merely careless about his language, Blackmur traces Lawrence's difficulties in writing good poetry back to the man's psychology—that is, back to his imbalance of mind.

Beginning with a definition, Blackmur states that the best poetry "has a rational structure which controls, orders, and composes in external or objective form the material of which it is made; and for that effect it is dependent only upon the craft and conventions of the art of poetry and upon the limits of language."[30] This is another formulation of Blackmur's belief that reason organizes the poet's feelings into forms without which poetry cannot be made intelligible. And the expression of these forms depends upon the conventions of poetry and of language. Because reason organizes feelings, or the material of poetry, into forms, then, Blackmur says, every poem should therefore have a rational structure. Lawrence's poetry fails, however, not only in the conventions of craft, but also because it lacks a rational structure which, to Blackmur, indicates a failure of mind. "The strength of his peculiar insight," Blackmur continues, "lacks the protection and support of a rational imagination, and it fails to its own disadvantage to employ the formal devices of the art in which it is couched." By "rational imagination" Blackmur means

some all-embracing view of philosophy of life by which
Lawrence could have ordered his experience and made it
intelligible.

According to Blackmur, Lawrence's lack of reason or "rational
imagination" resulted in hysteria, or "disproportionate reactions
to the shock of experience." Lawrence's reaction to life was not
to escape from it but to heighten and distort it "to a terrifying
and discomposing intensity." This intensity, Blackmur says, might
have produced great poetry if Lawrence could have controlled it
with his reason. Instead, like Cummings, he tried to express his
intense feelings directly, with the result that his poetry is
fragmentary and lacking in meaning. Blackmur says of Lawrence
that he "submitted the obsessions of his experience to the
heightening fire of hysteria and put down the annealed product
just as it came."

Blackmur's opinion is that some of Lawrence's poetry suc-
ceeds, however, because of the universal nature of its subject
matter and the honesty of his observations. In Lawrence's
observations it is "the very irreducible surd that makes the
hysteria an affair of genius not of insanity." To illustrate
Lawrence's failure and his success in writing poetry, Blackmur
quotes the concluding lines from "Tortoise Shout."

> The cross,
> The wheel on which our silence first is broken,
> Sex, which breaks up our integrity, our single
>   inviolability, our deep silence,
> Tearing a cry from us.
>
> Sex, which breaks us into voice, sets us calling
>   across the deeps, calling, calling for the
>   complement,
> Singing and calling, and singing again, being
>   answered, having found,
> Torn, to become whole again, after long seeking
>   what is lost
> The same cry from the tortoise as from Christ,
>   the Osiris-cry of abandonment,
> That which is whole, torn asunder,
> That which is in part, finding its whole again
>   throughout the universe.

These lines are indicative, Blackmur says, of Lawrence's inclination toward a certain kind of experience which he identifies as "the sexual, emergent character of all life: and in terms of that bias, which is the controlling principle, the seed of reality, in the hysteria of expression, Lawrence brings every notation and association, every symbolic suggestion he can find, to bear upon the shrieking plasm of the self." In Blackmur's view, insofar as "Tortoise Shout" reaches the condition of "ritual, formal or declarative prayer and mystical identification," it is successful. But on the whole the poem fails because "the ordering of words in component rhythms, the array of rhymes for prediction, contrast, transition and suspense, the delay of ornament, the anticipation of the exactly situated dramatic trope, the development of image and observation to an inevitable end—the devices which make a poem cohere, move, and shine apart—these are mostly not here, or are present badly and at fault." Blackmur goes on to say that because Lawrence did not pay enough attention to the craft of poetry, he deprived himself of any external criterion by which he could measure his inner demon. And that, Blackmur says, "is the fallacy of the faith in expressive form—the faith some aspects of which we have been discussing, that if a thing is only intensely enough felt its mere expression in words will give it satisfactory form, the dogma, in short, that once material becomes words it is its own best form." Great poetry, on the other hand, is composed on "the principle that the reality of language, which is a formal medium of knowledge, is superior and anterior to the reality of the uses to which it is put, and [on] the operative principle, that the chaos of private experience cannot be known or understood until it is projected and ordered in a form external to the consciousness that entertained it in flux."

In Blackmur's critical canon, words have meaning before they are used by the poet. The poet's reason and imagination must take these meanings into account when he attempts to express his experience. The relationship between words and the poet's experience should be one of mutual benefit. Words give expression to the poet's experience and the poet's experience should give the conventional forms of language new life. When this relationship is denied or through ignorance not taken into account, the words the poet uses will seem "flat" and will communicate only so much meaning as they themselves have, prior to their use by the poet. And this, to Blackmur, is the characteristic fault in Lawrence's poetry. Even where his poetry is successful in communicating meaning, his success depends "not so much on his bare statements, as upon the constant function of communication which cannot be expunged from the language."

C. Hart Crane[31]

Crane's problem, says Blackmur, is that he does not infuse his language with enough of his private experience to delimit the possible meanings inherent in the words he uses. To understand what Crane means, the reader must "supply from outside the poem, and with the help of clues only, the important, *controlling* part of what may be loosely called the meaning." To illustrate, Blackmur chooses a stanza from Crane's poem "The Wine Menagerie."

> New thresholds, new anatomies! Wine talons
> Build freedom up about me and distill
> This competence—to travel in a tear
> Sparkling alone, within another's will.

The first phrase is an example of Crane's working habit with words. He takes, Blackmur states, two totally unrelated words, "thresholds," and "anatomies"; and, by juxtaposing them, he creates a new synthesis of meaning. "We see that thresholds open upon anatomies; upon things to be explored and understood and felt freshly as an adventure; and we see that the anatomies, what is to be explored, are known from a new vantage, and that the vantage is part of the anatomy. The separate meanings of the words fairly rush at each other; the right ones join and those irrelevant to the juncture are for the moment—the whole time of the poem—lost in limbo." "Wine talons," however, retains too much of its own meaning. That is, it retains too many possible meanings because there is no help from the rest of the poem to aid the reader in determining Crane's meaning: "the possibilities have among them none specially discriminated, and whichever you choose for use, the dead weight of the others must be provisionally carried along, which is what makes the phrase slightly fuzzy."

This same problem is present in another of Crane's poems, "Lachrymae Christi."

> (Let sphinxes from the ripe
> Borage of death have cleared my tongue
> Once and again . . .)

Part of the difficulty in these lines, Blackmur says, is syntactical. "Let" is used as an adjective having the possible meanings of "neglected or weary, permitted or prevented, hired, and let in the sense that blood is let." Sphinxes are those inscrutable half-man, half-lion creatures that propound unanswerable riddles. "Borage" may mean "something rough (sonally suggestive of barrage and barrier); a blue-flowered, hairy-leaved plant, and a cordial made from the plant." But what Crane might have meant by putting these words together is problematical. Perhaps the meaning is "something to the effect that if you meditate enough on death it has the same bracing and warming effect as drinking a cordial, so that the riddles of life (or death) are answered. But something very near the contrary may have been intended; or both. In any case, a guess is ultimately worthless because, with the defective syntax, the words do not verify it." Therefore, Blackmur continues, Crane's basic poetic fault is that he could not consistently mask, obliterate, or suspend the other meanings of a word he did not want to include. He tried but failed to "produce a new and living, an idiomatic, meaning, differing from and surpassing the separate factors involved." And further, this fault is compounded by the fact that Crane had "the sensibility typical of Baudelaire and so misunderstood himself that he attempted to write *The Bridge* as if he had the sensibility typical of Whitman. He used the private lyric to write the cultural epic; used the mode of intensive contemplation, which secures ends, to present the mind's reactions, which have no ends. The confusion of tool and purpose not only led him astray in conceiving his themes; it obscured at crucial moments the exact character of the work he was actually doing."

In the terms of Blackmur's critical canon, Crane, Lawrence, and Cummings try to express their feelings directly without using their reason to find forms for their feelings or to find words to adequately express those forms. Wallace Stevens, W. B. Yeats, and T. S. Eliot, on the other hand, are poets whose poetry shows evidence of a controlling reason without loss of intensity.

D. *Wallace Stevens*

Blackmur particularly likes Stevens's "double adherence to words and experience as existing apart from his private sensibility."[32] Stevens is able to maintain an objective distance when viewing his experience because his reason plays its full part in the poetic process and the evidence can be seen in his language. In Blackmur's view, Stevens's appreciation and respect for words give to his poetry a precision that none of the three poets previously discussed was able to reach. Furthermore, Stevens has the knack for continually combining words into new syntheses of meaning.

Stevens is able to effect such new combinations by an extreme fidelity "to the individual words as they appear in the dictionary." Because Stevens is extremely faithful to the meanings of individual words, he can communicate through his poetry precise emotions which "can be truly perceived only in the form of words in which [they are] given." To put it differently, the words become the emotion the poet is seeking to express. Blackmur cites two linguistic examples to illustrate his point: "Funest philosophers" and "Fubbed the girandoles."

"Funest," Blackmur says, is derived from a French word meaning "fatal, melancholy, baneful, and has to do with death and funerals." "Funest" is better than any other word Stevens could have used because it is the "essence of the funeral in its sadness, not its sadness alone, that makes it the right word: the clouds are going to their death, as not only philosophers but less indoctrinated ponderers know; so what they say, what they evoke, in pondering, has that much in common with the clouds." "Funest" is also the right word in terms of the preceding lines and "the statement about their evocations is central to the poem and illuminates it. The word pomps, above, means ceremony and comes from a Greek word meaning procession, often, by association, a funeral, as in the phrase funeral pomps. So the pomps of the clouds suggests the funeral in funest." The stanza from "On the Manner of Addressing Clouds" that Blackmur has been working with is:

> Gloomy grammarians in golden gowns,
> Meekly you keep the mortal rendezvous,
> Eliciting the still sustaining pomps

> Of speech which are like music so profound
> They seem an exhaltation without sound.
> Funest philsophers and ponderers,
> Their evocations are the speech of clouds.

"Fubbed the girandoles" (meaning, outshone the chandeliers) offers a different kind of precision in language and is in the third stanza of "The Ordinary Women."

> Then from their poverty they rose,
> From dry catarrhs, and to guitars
> They flitted
> Through the palace walls.
>
> They flung monotony behind
> Turned from their want, and, nonchalant,
> They crowded
> The nocturnal halls.
>
> The lacquered loges huddled there
> Mumbled zay-zay and a-zay-a-zay
> The moonlight
> Fubbed the girandoles.

The precision in these words, Blackmur says, is the balance they maintain between sound and sense.

Somewhere between the realms of ornamental sound and representative statement, the words pause and balance, dissolve and resolve. This is the mood of *Euphues*, and presents a poem with fine parts controlled internally by little surds of feeling that save both the poem and its parts from preciousness. The ambiguity of this sort of writing consists in the double importance of both sound and sense where neither has direct connection with the other but where neither can stand alone. It is as if Mr. Stevens wrote two poems at once with the real poem somewhere between, unwritten but valid.

The balance the words of this poem maintain is due to the unity of sensibility a good poet needs to write good poetry. On the other hand, the words have meaning in the context of the poem which goes beyond the meaning they have by themselves as words independent of the poetic structure. And this meaning the words have in the context of the poem is due to, or rather is controlled by, Stevens's reason since this is the faculty responsible for the choice of words that will represent the poet's experience. On the other hand, Stevens's imagination has given his choice of words a vividness and intensity that parallels, Blackmur feels, the vividness and intensity of Stevens's original experience. Neither the intensity reflected by the words nor their meaning can be separated from imagination. When reason and imagination are unified so that they cannot be separated, the result, Blackmur says, is the establishment in the reader of an "interior experience" that parallels the experience felt by the poet. Blackmur's remarks on another of Stevens's poems, "Sea Surface Full of Clouds," are illustrative. The particular lines of the poem he refers to are: "Then the sea / And heaven rolled as one and from the two / Came fresh transfigurings of freshest blue." "Here we have words," he says, "used as a tone of feeling to secure the discursive evanescence of appearances; words bringing the senses into the mind which they created; the establishment of interior experience by the construction of its tone in words."

The construction of the "tone" of experience depends upon the balance between the poet's reason and imagination—his sensibility. Reason finds the forms (language) for the poet's experience while imagination infuses the chosen words with the intensity of the original experience. So the "tone of feeling" Blackmur refers to is the evidence in a poem that the poet's reason and imagination are in balance and cannot be separated. This is the point of Blackmur's remark that "Mr. Stevens is a genuine poet in that he attempts constantly to transform what is felt with the senses and what is thought in the mind—if we can still distinguish the two—into that realm of being, which we call poetry, where what is thought is felt and what is felt has the strict point of thought." There is, finally, in Stevens's poetry a blending of thought and feeling, sound and sense, reason and imagination that fulfills Blackmur's criterion of unified sensibility.

E. W. B. Yeats[33]

Blackmur's interest in the poetry of William Butler Yeats centers on the poet's philosophy. In Blackmur's critical canon, reason makes experience meaningful by ordering it according to the poet's philosophy of life. In Yeats's poetry, magic, Blackmur says, is the philosophy of life by which experience is made intelligible. "Magic performs for Yeats the same fructifying function that Christianity does for Eliot, or that ironic fatalism did for Thomas Hardy; it makes a connection between the poem and its subject matter and provides an adequate mechanics of meaning and value." Magic is not only a controlling principle for Yeats's experience but also "the ultimate mode for the apprehension of reality." This, says Blackmur, places a double burden on Yeats. He must consistently utilize the conventions he finds to express his experience, and he must restore in his conventions "through the *craft* of poetry, both the reality and its symbols to that plane where alone their experience becomes actual—the plane of the quickened senses and the concrete emotions." To put it a different way, Yeats's reason must use the conventions of language consistently and his imagination must then infuse these conventions with the vividness and the vitality of his original experience. Or, still another way, if the poet is going to use images and symbols that are not traditionally related to the emotions he wishes to express in his poetry, then he must use those images and symbols consistently so that an understandable relationship is built up; in effect, the poet must establish the poetical equivalent of musical leitmotifs.

The specific artistic problem in Yeats's poetry is his use of magic as a way of making his experience meaningful. In Blackmur's view, the use of magic is a very personal and idiosyncratic way of ordering one's experience. He means that magic is not, in the twentieth century, part of the general cultural experience. The linguistic conventions that Yeats derives from his magic are not likely to be known by ordinary readers. Therefore, Blackmur says, Yeats must explain his "doctrines at the same time that he represents their emotional or dramatic equivalents." In this respect Yeats finds himself "in much the same position that Dante would have been had he had to construct his Christian doctrine while he was composing *The Divine Comedy:* an impossible labor." Yeats cannot expect that his readers will comprehend his conception of magic because the "knowledge and power" of magic "can neither be generally shared nor overtly rationalized." Yeats has described his conception of magic in his *A Vision,* but this book is not generally well known, Blackmur continues, and thus the average reader has difficulty understanding the rationale behind the poetry.

A problem related to Yeats's use of magical images and symbols is that the kind of poetry he writes promises knowledge it cannot give: "It promises, as in 'The Second Coming,' exact prediction of events in the natural world; and it promises again and again, in different poems, exact revelations of the supernatural." But Yeats's poetry does not, in fact, give predictions or revelations but a sense of "the exaltation in his language." Blackmur means that Yeats's poetry does not convey his *understanding* or knowledge of the supernatural—only his sense of revelation. In Blackmur's critical canon, the meaningfulness of the language conventions the poet chooses depends upon the correct use of his reason. To Blackmur, Yeats's poetry does not have a "rational superstructure that persists and which we can convert to our own modes if we will." Blackmur suggests two possible remedies for this problem. The reader may convert Yeats's magic and the conventions by which he expresses it into a psychological framework because Yeats's magic and psychology "have so much in common"; or Yeats's magic may be accepted "literally as a machinery of meaning, [leaving the reader the task of discovering] the prose parallels and reconstruct[ing] the symbols he uses on their own terms in order to come on the emotional reality, if it is there, actually in the poems—when the machinery may be dispensed with." Blackmur is quick to point out that with either remedy the critic doctors "himself as much as Yeats." Even so, either remedy will serve to point to the unity of sensibility in Yeats's work and to the creative energy of his mind, Blackmur says.

"Leda and the Swan," for instance, can be read on three levels: "the levels of dramatic fiction, of condensed insight into Greek mythology, and a third level of fiction and insight combined, as we said, to represent and hide a magical insight." Blackmur goes on to say that in the image of the swan Yeats has found an image to express the emotion of an insight that has its origins in magic. Since the swan is also part of a myth, the myth too becomes a correlative for the insight. But, Blackmur cautions, "It is a neat question for the reader, so far as this poem is concerned, whether the poetic emotion springs from the doctrine and seizes the myth for a safe home and hiding, or whether the doctrine is correlative to the emotion of the myth." Finally, Blackmur writes, Yeats worked into his poetry the substance of Irish mythology and Irish politics and gave them a symbolism, and he developed his experience with Theosophy and Rosicrucianism into a body of conventions adequate, for him, to animate the concrete poetry of the soul that he wished to write. He did not do these things separately; the mythology, the politics, and the magic are conceived, through the personalities that reflected them, with an increasing unity of apprehension. Thus more than any poet of our time he has restored to poetry the actual emotions of race and religion and what we call abstract thought.

F.   T. S. Eliot[34]

To Blackmur, T. S. Eliot's religion is one of the most important aspects of his poetry. "Now a man's religion is the last thing we can take for granted about him" Blackmur writes, "Which is as it should be; and when a writer shows the animating presence of religion in his work, and to the advantage of his work, the nature of that presence and its linkage deserve our earnest examination." Blackmur is particularly interested in "the problem of the moral and technical validity of Mr. Eliot's Christianity as it labours to seize the actual for representation in his poetry." Eliot's poetry is "penetrated and animated and its significance is determined by Christian feeling, and especially by the Christian distinction of Good and Evil . . . the Church is in Mr. Eliot's poetry his view of life; it recognizes and points [out] the issues and shapes their poetic course; it is the rationale of his drama and the witness of its fate; it is, in short, a way of handling poetic material to its best advantage."

Eliot's experience, Blackmur writes, as it is presented, for instance, in "Ash Wednesday," is meaningful only when it is read in a theological context. The abnegation in the first part of the poem is Christian abnegation "whereby you give up what you can of the evil of the flesh for the good of the soul." In terms of Blackmur's poetics, Eliot's reason has chosen the convention of Christian abnegation to make his own feelings of self-denial meaningful. Similarly, Blackmur says, the words of Arnaut Daniel quoted in the fourth section of "Ash Wednesday" gain their full significance only when "the force of the Christian teaching" is recognized.

To Blackmur, Eliot's religion serves as a source of symbols and images for his poetry and also makes Eliot's entire life experience meaningful. The emotions that have been traditionally associated with religion—emotions like sacrifice, belief, and piety—are used by Eliot as conventions to express similar feelings. Also, Blackmur says, religion gives to Eliot's poetry an air of authority and experience well understood and organized. "The Church is the vehicle through which human purpose is to be seen and its teachings prod and vitalise the poetic sensibility engaged with the actual and with the substrata of the actual. Furthermore, and directly for poetry, the Church presents a gift of moral and philosophical form of a pre-logical character; and it is a great advantage for a poet to find his material fitting into a form whose reason is in mystery rather than logic, and no less reason for that."

Finally, readers of Eliot have to make an imaginative recovery of the animating force of religion because, Blackmur believes, religion is no longer part of our living heritage. In other words, the passions, the intellectual problems, the special psychology associated with a life lived in the service of the Church or with a life lived constantly in the shadow of the Church, are replaced by other passions, problems, and psychologies.

III   *Summary*

Generally speaking, the essays on E. E. Cummings, Hart Crane, and Wallace Stevens focus their critical attention upon the words of selected poems, while the essays on the poetry of D. H. Lawrence, W. B. Yeats, and T. S. Eliot emphasize these poets' attitude to life or their life's controlling principle. A characteristic of all six essays is that the poem is never considered apart from the poet. Indeed, Blackmur tells us as much about the minds of his subjects as he does about their poetry. This is not unusual if it is granted that in Blackmur's poetics the poem is the result of a creative process that is highly important to the success or failure of that poem. What is unusual about Blackmur's criticism of poetry is the extended field of operation he seems to envisage for poetry.

Earlier in this chapter I mentioned that the poem in Blackmur's poetics is an intermediary in the communication between poet and audience. As can be deduced from the essays just reviewed, the poem, to Blackmur, is also something more.

The poem is also the center of a social nexus which includes the poet, the audience, and all the institutions of society. Although Blackmur does not explicitly state that poetry is a social phenomenon, he treats it as such in his criticism. This social aspect of poetry may also be deduced from his assumption that a poem should be understood by someone other than the poet himself. Since understanding in that case would involve at least two people, and these two people do not exist in a vacuum, the poem can be said to have social significance. Simply speaking, Blackmur treats poetry as a means of communication having social significance in much the same way as one can talk about a telephone both as a mechanical instrument and as a powerful force molding the habits of society.

Treating the poem as a social phenomenon allows Blackmur to widen his critical scope. His method is to consider the poem as a symptomatic expression of the collective mind of society. In the actual composition of his essays, however, he may begin either with the poet, or the poem, or society in general. In his essay on Cummings, for instance, he begins with the poet himself. "Mr. Cummings is a school of writing in himself, so that it is necessary to state the underlying assumptions of his mind, and of the school which he teaches, before dealing with the specific results in poetry of those assumptions." Not much further into the essay, Blackmur mentions one of the consequences of the antiintellectual school of poetry. "The central attitude of this group has developed, in its sectaries, a logical and thoroughgoing set of principles and habits. . . . These dogmas have been defended with considerable dialectical skill, on the very practiced premise that only by presenting the unintelligible as viable and actual *per se* can the culture of the *dead intelligence* (Brattle Street, the Colleges, and the Reviews) be shocked into sentience."

From this outburst Blackmur goes on to his analysis of Cummings's language. The order might just as well be reversed as it is in the Stevens essay, or he could have begun with society, then gone on to the poet, and finally to the poem—the order of the Crane essay. At the end of the first paragraph of the Crane essay Blackmur writes: "Light, radiance, and wholeness remain the attributes of serious art. And the fact is disheartening because no time could have greater need than our own for rational art. No time certainly could surrender more than ours does daily, with drums beating, to fanatic politics and despotically construed emotions." Here we have a capsule formulation of the state of society, and it is interesting to note the connection Blackmur makes between "rational art" and social conditions. Although it has not been stressed in this chapter because it is more developed in his later work, Blackmur had an Arnoldian hope for the restorative, curative powers art might bring to society.

As a critic, then, Blackmur draws conclusions about society from his analyses of poetry and vice versa. Often, however, it is difficult to tell from which source Blackmur is drawing his conclusions. In his essay on Eliot, for example, it is difficult to say whether Blackmur's belief that Christianity is no longer a living tradition has its source in Eliot's poetry or in some general assessment of society to which Eliot's poetry happens to conform. But no matter, the point is that to Blackmur, from the very beginning of his career, poetry and society were inextricably interconnected. Poetry imposes upon society "a deep reminder of a part of our heritage which we have lost except for the stereotypes of spiritual manners" and the conditions of society impose upon the poet the need to find some principle of life by which his experience can be ordered.

The spiritual health of society has an important influence on Blackmur's criticism of poetry and that influence becomes greater and stronger as his career progresses. But even in the relatively early essays on Yeats and Eliot, Blackmur focuses his critical attention on the conditions of society which make necessary the almost mechanical adoption of an artificial or moribund world-view. "Poetry does not flow from thin air but requires always either a literal faith, an imaginative faith, or, as in Shakespeare a mind full of many provisional faiths. The life we all live is not alone enough of a subject for the serious artist; it must be a life with a leaning, life with a tendency to shape itself only in certain forms, to afford its most lucid revelations only in certain lights." To Blackmur, life in the twentieth century cannot be by itself the subject of serious artistic interest because it lacks the moral direction and intellectual sustaining force that is needed to make poetry meaningful in terms of which the whole of Western culture can be understood. Blackmur shares, in this regard, Matthew Arnold's world-view, except that Blackmur attributes the loss of shared cultural values to more than the decline of religion. In Blackmur's view, all the value-giving institutions of society have declined; hence, the need of poets like Yeats and Eliot to find their own world-view and their consequent responsibility to explain it to their audience—if, in Blackmur's view, they want to have an audience.

Finally, the relationship between poetry and society in Dante's time and in our own serves, for Blackmur, as a defining contrast. "Dante," he writes,

completed for poetry the Christian culture of his time, which was itself the completion of centuries. But there was at hand for Dante, and as a rule in the great ages of poetry, a fundamental agreement or convention between the poet and his audience about the validity of the view of life of which the poet deepened the reality and spread the scope. There is no such agreement today. We find poets either using the small conventions of the individual life as if they were great conventions, or attempting to resurrect some great convention of the past, or, finally, attempting to discover the great convention that must lie, willy-nilly, hidden in the life about them.[35]

The relationship between poetry and society is reciprocal. Society gives, or should give to the poet the means for expressing his private experience in images and symbols that bespeak a unified and homogeneous culture. The poet, on the other hand, widens and deepens society's understanding of its collective experience.

CHAPTER 3

The Role of the Critic

BLACKMUR is probably best known for his essays on the critical process. At least one, "A Critic's Job of Work," has attained the status of a classic. In that particular essay he focuses his attention on the critical process. In later essays he enlarges his focus to include considerations of the social role of the critic. The five essays that I will consider in this chapter cover the full range of Blackmur's criticism of criticism.

I "A Critic's Job of Work"

"A Critic's Job of Work" is Blackmur's earliest published essay on criticism.[1] In this essay Blackmur makes a number of unstated assumptions that are important to an understanding of his criticism. Blackmur assumes that every critic has a mind, with reason and imagination having somewhat separate but complementary functions. The function of reason, in Blackmur's description, is to elicit facts from the work under review and then to ascertain their meaning by creating a meaningful order for them. The critic's reason creates this order by relating the facts of a work to the critical method the critic employs. Thus the meaning the facts contained in a work will have depends on the critical method used. In the same way, the meaning the poet's reason creates out of his experience depends on the poet's philosophy of life. In Blackmur's view, a philosophy of life is analogous to a critical method.

The work of art, Blackmur says, is composed of facts which the critic's reason must try to discover. A fact is anything that may be stated about a work—its structure, its theme, its meaning, its rhythm, and so on. But Blackmur continues, "facts are not simple or easy to come at; not all the facts will appear to one mind, and the same facts appear differently in the light of different minds.

No attention is undivided, no single approach sufficient, no predilection guaranteed, when facts or what their arrangements create are in question." The work is composed of facts, the understanding of which depends on the perceptiveness of the individual critic. And since one mind cannot take in all the facts, Blackmur implies that, for any given critic, part of the work will remain a mystery. That is, the critic's reason will not be able to ascertain the full meaning of the work. The meaning the critic is able to ascertain using his reason will depend on his critical method. Unfortunately, Blackmur writes, the methods that can be applied "are as various as the heresies of the Christian Church, and like them testify to occasional needs, fanatic emphasis, special interest, or intellectual pride, all flowing from and even the worst of them enlightening the same body of insight." But, he continues, "just as heresies tend to restore vitality to orthodoxy, different critical methods tend to restore vitality to individual perception. The danger lies in accepting any one critical method as sufficient and final. As soon as method becomes dogma, it "must fall the moment too much weight is laid upon it—the moment, in short, it is taken literally." And this usually happens to a critical method, Blackmur says, because for most minds "the doctrinal mode of thinking seems the only one possible." However, "no form, no formula of knowledge ought to be surrendered merely because it runs the risk in bad or desperate hands of being used literally; and similarly, in our own thinking, whether it is carried to the point of formal discourse or not, we cannot afford, we ought scrupulously to risk the use of any concept that is propitious or helpful in getting over gaps."

Any critical method should be used "consciously, provisionally, speculatively, and dramatically." The terms of any critical method should be used "for their own sakes alone and with only a pious or ritualistic regard for the doctrines in which they are clothed." In other words, the critic should avoid the illogic and inconsistencies that are inherently part of any doctrine in using the terms of that same doctrine for his own critical purposes. For example, Blackmur continues, the doctrine of solipsism "because of the logical doctrine prepared to support it, technical philosophers will employ years to get around the impasse in which it leaves them; whereas men of poetic imagination merely use it for the dramatic insight it contains." The critic, then, should borrow from every doctrine he knows, taking what he needs and leaving the rest. But is it possible to apply the borrowed terms without taking along with them at least some of the doctrines also? Or does the critic use his borrowed terms under the aegis of his own critical methodology? If so, may it then be said that the critic's own critical principles form part of what may be called his critical doctrine; and that he is merely moving terms from one doctrine to another? To answer these questions Blackmur writes that "fortunately, there exist archetypes of unindoctrinated thinking." Unindoctrinated thinking is thinking with the "absence of positive doctrine," and Blackmur finds such thinking in "the early Plato and the whole Montaigne." Plato's dramatic irony and Montaigne's imaginative scepticism are "the only rational approach to the multiplication of doctrines and arrogant technologies which fills out the body of critical thinking." Blackmur admires the way Plato "always holds conflicting ideas in shifting balance, presenting them in contest and evolution" and the way Montaigne "is always making room for another idea, and implying a third for provisional, adjudicating irony." Adopting both Plato's method of juggling ideas and Montaigne's method of keeping an ironic sense of their value keeps "the mind athletic and the spirit on the stretch." This is the critical point of view, Blackmur says, in which terms borrowed from other doctrines should be used. If the critic keeps to the spirit of Plato and Montaigne, his criticism will not become stultifying dogma; instead, his criticism will remain undoctrinaire and flexible.

If, instead of just borrowing terms, a critic adopts a whole doctrine for a critical method, the adoption should be made with a clear understanding of the limitations of the doctrine. "What produces the evil of stultification and the malice of controversy is the confused approach, when the limits are not seen because they tend to cancel each other out, and the driving power becomes emotional." In Blackmur's opinion, something like this happened to Irving Babbitt. Because Babbitt had no idea of the limitations of his method, gross distortions occurred in his criticism. Babbitt and a colleague, Paul Elmer More, were outspoken defenders of a particular critical methodology in the 1920s. The methodology was called humanism, with no capital letter, and was loosely based upon classical criteria. It was used by Babbitt and More, in Blackmur's view, without regard to the special literary needs and insights of Blackmur's generation. In "A Critic's Job of Work" Blackmur uses Babbitt as an example of a particular kind of critic who used his critical approach without an awareness of its methodological limitations.

Even though, in Blackmur's opinion, Babbitt's critical methodology caused serious misreadings of modern literature, there is, however, some value to be found. "Once we reduce . . . the magnitude of application of such notions as the inner check and the higher will, which were for Babbitt paramount,—that is, when we determine the limits within which he really worked— then the massive erudition and acute observation with which his work is packed become permanently available." Keeping Babbitt in mind as a contrasting example, Blackmur argues that the best critic

keeps his criticism from becoming either instinctive or vicarious, and the labour of his understanding is always specific, like the art he examines; and he knows that the sum of his best work comes only to the pedagogy of elucidation and appreciation. He observes facts and he delights in discriminations. The object remains, and should remain, itself, only made more available and seen in a clearer light.

Because the meaning a work will have depends so much on the method of critical analysis, Blackmur continues his essay with comments on six representative critical methods.

George Santayana's method in his essay on Lucretius in *Three Philosophical Poets* is to convert a "poetic ordering of nature to the terms of a moral philosophy." In Blackmur's opinion, Santayana's critical method has changed the meaning of Lucretius to reflect his own moral bias.

In his *The Pilgrimage of Henry James,* Van Wyck Brooks has taken art "not as the objectification or mirroring of social experience but as a personal expression and escape-fantasy of the artist's personal life in dramatic extension." Brooks takes the theme of the tragedy of the unsuccessful artist and "raises it to an obsession, an omnivorous concept, under which all other themes can be subsumed." The result, Blackmur says, is that Brooks distorts the meaning of James's work.

Granville Hicks's critical method distorts the meaning of a whole body of American literature. In Hicks's *The Great Tradition,* criticism reaches "to the point where the travail of judgment is suspended and becomes the mere reiteration of a formula." Hicks, says Blackmur, "is not writing criticism at all; he is writing a fanatic's history and a casuist's polemic."

The common critical fault of Santayana, Brooks, and Hicks is that they all "leave literature so soon behind" in their single-minded approaches. While any critical method is bound to distort meaning to some extent, it will distort less if it remains in "sustained contact" with the work. "We have constantly—if our interest is really in literature—to prod ourselves back, to remind ourselves that there was a poem, a play, or a novel of some initial and we hope terminal concern, or we have to falsify facts and set up fictions to the effect that no matter what we are saying we are really talking about art after all." But remaining in sustained contact with a work of art does not guarantee a minimum of distortion. In Blackmur's view, the critical methods of I. A. Richards, Kenneth Burke, and S. Foster Damon keep the work in focus at all times, yet each distorts meaning beyond acceptable limits.

I. A. Richards is a critic who must "deliberately expand the theoretic phase of every practical problem." In Richards's work, Blackmur writes,

there is a tendency to urge the scientific principle and the statistical method, and in doing so to bring in the whole assorted world of thought. That Mr. Richards, who is an admirable critic and whose love and knowledge of poetry are incontestable, is a victim of the expansiveness of his mind in these directions, is what characterizes, and reduces, the scope of his work in literary criticism.

Richards's theoretical constructs are so "vast, so labyrinthine, so inclusive" that the amount "of actual literary criticism is so small that it seems almost a by-product instead of the central product." Richards is really interested in his critical method for its own sake and not in what it can tell him about literature. Richards's readers, Blackmur says, must learn "the enormous variety and complexity of the operations possible in the process of verbally describing and defining brief passages of imaginative language and the equal variety and complexity of the result; you learn the practical impossibility of verbally ascertaining what the author means—and you hear nothing of the other ways of apprehending meaning at all." In short, Richards's critical method stultifies "the very power it was aimed to enhance—the power of imaginative apprehension, of imaginative coordination of varied and separable elements." And further, Richards's method seriously distorts meaning because it does not take into account that part of meaning which depends on the critic's intuition. "Because it is possible," Blackmur continues,

to apply scientific methods to the language of poetry, and because scientific methods engross their subject matter, Mr. Richards places the whole burden of criticism in the application of a scientific approach, and asserts it to be an implement for the judgment of poetry. Actually it can handle only the language and its words and cannot touch—except by assertion—the imaginative product of the words which is the poetry: which is the object revealed or elucidated by criticism.

Kenneth Burke uses his critical method in the same way that Richards uses his—as an end rather than as a means. Instead of keeping his critical focus on the work and its possible meanings, Blackmur writes, Burke uses the work "not only as a springboard but also as a resort or home, for a philosophy or psychology of moral possibility." Burke is "more interested in the psychological means of the meaning, and how it might mean (and often really does) something else, than in the meaning itself."

S. Foster Damon's *William Blake* is an example of scholarship as a critical method. Blackmur defines scholarship as the "collection, arrangement, and scrutiny of facts." As a critical method, scholarship, in Blackmur's opinion, never goes far enough in its investigations into the work because once the facts have been elicted from the work, there is never any subsequent attempt to explain what the collected facts might mean; that is, scholarship does not attempt to "investigate the mysteries of meaning or to connect literature with other departments of life—it has only to furnish the factual materials for such investigations and connections." Scholarship does not overly distort meaning largely because it is not concerned with it. Scholarship, however, prepares the way for interpretation and

must be done to the appropriate degree of digging out the facts in all orders of poetry—and especially perhaps in contemporary poetry, where we tend to let the work go either because it seems too easy or because it seems supererogatory. Self-evident facts are paradoxically the hardest to come by; they are not evident till they are seen; yet the meaning of a poem—the part of it which is intellectually formulable— must invariably depend on this order of facts, the facts about the meanings of the elements aside from their final meaning in combination.

The rest of the poem, what it is, what it shows, its final value as a created emotion, its meanings, if you like, *as* a poem, cannot in the more serious orders of poetry develop itself to the full without this factual or intellectual meaning to show the way.

Having commented on the inadequacies of six critical methodologies, Blackmur goes on to mention that his own critical method is a technical one which "does not tell the whole story either." His approach to literary criticism is "primarily through the technique, in the widest sense of that word, of the examples handled; technique on the plane of words and even of linguistics in Mr. Richards's sense, but also technique on the plane of intellectual and emotional patterns in Mr. Burke's sense, and technique, too, in that there is a technique of securing and arranging and representing a fundamental view of life." Blackmur adds that

the advantage of the technical approach is, I think, double. It readily admits other approaches and is anxious to be complemented by them. Furthermore, in a sense, it is able to incorporate the technical aspect, which always exists, with what is secured by other approaches—as I have argued elsewhere that so unpromising a matter as T. S. Eliot's religious convictions may be profitably considered as a dominant element in his technique of revealing the actual. The second advantage of the technical approach is a consequence of the first; it treats of nothing in literature except in its capacity of reduction to literary fact, which is where it resembles scholarship, only passing beyond it in that its facts are usually further into the heart of the literature than the facts of most scholarship.

Blackmur has adopted the technical method because "it can go the furthest" into the heart of the work. But, he cautions, "mere technical scrutiny of any order, is not enough without direct apprehension—which may come first or last—to which all scrutinies that show facts contribute." Imaginative or direct apprehension must also be a relevant part of the critical act because it is only "the facts about a poem, a play, a novel, that can be reduced to tractable form, talked about, and examined; the rest is the product of the facts, from the technical point of view. The rest, whatever it is, can only be known, not talked about."

According to Blackmur's description, then, any work can be

divided into two major aspects which should each come under critical analysis. The first major aspect is what Blackmur calls the "facts" of the work. Only these facts, he says, can be talked about in critical analysis. The rest, or what remains after the facts have been discovered is Ransom's X—that incremental phenomenon that makes a work more than the sum of its parts, and which can only be "known" or intuited by the critic. At this stage of his career, however, Blackmur is concerned only with the critic's conscious activity.

The importance of "A Critic's Job of Work" lies in what it tells us about Blackmur's conception of the critical act as he envisioned it in 1935. First, according to Blackmur, the critic must have a certain attitude or habit of mind that he says is reflected in the "early Plato and whole Montaigne." That is, a critic should approach a work with imaginative scepticism and dramatic irony. Second, the critic should only focus upon the work in hand without what Blackmur calls "ulterior motives"; however, he says, if a critic must "concern himself with those purposes or with some one among them which obsess him, . . . he must further not assume except within the realm of his special argument that other purposes either do not exist or are negligible or that the works may not be profitably discussed apart from ulterior purposes and as examples of dramatic possibilities alone." Third, in confronting the work, the critic should do a job of scholarship which Blackmur defines as "the collection, arrangement, and scrutiny of facts." Once this is done, the critical act is not yet completed because the job of scholarship does not "investigate the mysteries of meaning or . . . connect literature with other departments of life—it has only to furnish the factual materials for such investigations and connections."

These three steps, even though they do not fully complete the critical act, comprise what Blackmur calls his own critical approach—the technical approach. However, he cautions, "my own approach, such as it is, and if it can be named, does not tell the whole story either; the reader is conscientiously left with the poem with the real work yet to do." And the real work of the critic, as well as of the reader, is the imaginative apprehension of the essence of the meaning that comes after the conscious gathering of facts. The imaginative apprehension completes the critical act. But what exactly is it and how does Blackmur include it in his description of the critical act?

At the time he wrote "The Critic's Job of Work," Blackmur had not as yet worked out how direct or imaginative apprehension was related to his technical approach to literature. "It may be," he mused, "that there are principles that cover both the direct apprehension and the labour of providing modes for the understanding of the expressive arts. If so, they are Socratic and found within, and subject to the fundamental scepticism as in Montaigne." This remark is important to an understanding of Blackmur's conception of the critical act. What the critic learns about a work through the technical approach is not all there is to be learned. There is more, Blackmur thinks, that may be learned only through direct apprehension. But how is direct apprehension achieved and what is it that the critic apprehends? In this essay under review, Blackmur gives only a partially satisfactory answer by introducing the "pre-conscious."

By intuition we adventure in the pre-conscious; and there, where the adventure is, there is no need or suspicion of certainty or meaning; there is the living expanding, *prescient* substance without the tags and handles of conscious form. Art is the looking glass of the pre-conscious, and when it is deepest seems to participate in it sensibly. Or, better, for purposes of criticism, our sensibility resumes the division of the senses and faculties at the same time that it preens itself into conscious form. Criticism may have as an object the establishment and evaluation (comparison and analysis) of the modes of making the pre-conscious *consciously* available.

Direct apprehension is achieved through the critic's intuition, understood in Blackmurian terms as an adventure in the preconscious. In the preconscious the work finally reveals itself to the critic as a "living, expanding *prescient* substance without the tags and handles of conscious form."

This is only a partial answer because the critic must find ways, as Blackmur himself admits, of establishing and evaluating the total work. It is interesting to observe, however, that intuition or imagination is definitely a part of the critical act.

By 1940, Blackmur calls the role of imagination in the critical act "the enabling act of criticism." In a short essay entitled "The Enabling Act of Criticism" he states that the critical act consists first, in being willing to concentrate your maximum attention upon the work which the words and the motions of the words—and by motions I mean all the technical devices of literature—perform upon each other. Secondly, it consists in submitting, at least provisionally, to whatever authority your attention brings to light in the words. In doing this you will be following in pretty close parallel the procedure which the writer followed. Whether your submission is permanent or must be withdrawn will be determined by the judgment of all the standards and all the interests you can bring to bear. These will differ with the work at hand. But the act of submission must be made before you can tell; it is an act of imagination, not of will; and it is the enabling act of criticism.[2]

When seen in the context of this statement, the emphasis in "The Critic's Job of Work" is on the first part of the critical act which is the conscious elucidation of the facts of a work. And in this first part of the critical act reason plays its role by creating order out of the mass of facts. The next essay emphasizes the role of imagination in the critical act.

II   *"Language As Gesture"*

"Language As Gesture" is Blackmur's best essay on the role of imagination in the critical act.[3] Since he uses the term "gesture" for the first time in this essay, I would like to begin by explaining its meaning in his critical thought. In Chapter 2 I mentioned that Blackmur calls the poet's reaction to the sense impressions that flux across his consciousness his "feelings." In Blackmur's critical canon, these sense impressions are of hearing, smell, taste, touch, sight, and of something that he variously calls "behavior," "life," "reality," "disorder," "the flux," and "gesture." All of these terms refer to the same concept. Blackmur adopts this concept for critical purposes and calls it "gesture."

In Blackmur's thought, gesture in poetry and the other arts is that added meaningfulness that cannot be accounted for by the analysis of the techniques of composition or by an analysis of the medium. Gesture can only be accounted for by the critic's imagination, although it can be circumstantially "proven" to be present by reference to compositional techniques and syntactic strategies. Gesture is directly analogous to the New Critics' "value" which they claim was somehow "anchored" in the structure of the poem. In "Language As Gesture," Blackmur attempts to describe what gesture is and how it may be proven to be present in art.

To begin with, gesture is a quality, or as Blackmur puts it, "that exited sense of being." The question is, how do we become aware of gesture in the arts? Blackmur's answer is that gesture makes itself felt through the various mediums of art. Taking church spires as an example, Blackmur says that gesture gives the "good" spire "the sense of movement, of aspiration, as a tree or a shrub gives the sense of process of growth, or as a beautiful room gives the effect of extending space rather than enclosing it." Continuing with his examples, Blackmur mentions that in sculpture gesture is that sense of "the moment arrested, in the moving stillness . . . at the moment of its greatest significance." Gesture in painting, at least in portrait painting, is "the single focal moment . . . of some particular state, some long perspective—say the lifelong heaviness of the head upon its little fulcrum—some deep inspiration of the flesh, say the desire *in weariness* for rest, or even, say, just the gaiety and radiance of the features in play with life." Gesture manifests itself in the dance as an aspect of its ritualistic nature. It is "the stable *and* moving element in ritual; it is both what is autochthonous— reborn out of the native soil of feeling—and what is autonomous—and independently controls the meaningfulness of ritual." Gesture in the dance is "the natural wayward play of the body controlled." Gesture in acting is similarly manifested. In acting it is "the purposive, conventional control of the body's movements . . . a kind of reduction, condensation, telescoping, of free instinctual movements." Gesture in dancing and acting is more readily apparent, Blackmur says, because it is manifested visually. But in music gesture is most apparent because music "alone of the arts can proceed according to its own purpose without either anterior or subsequent obligation to any other art." The forms of music lead to gesture, and, in the best music, gesture is form. The musician's "form and his substance will be united in process as well as at the end: united as gesture."

This identity of form and content gives to music its power and its intensity of expression. Similarly in all the arts gesture "is what happens to a form when it becomes identical with its subject." In poetry, whose medium is language, gesture is "the outward and dramatic play of inward and imaged meaning. It is that play of meaningfulness among words which cannot be defined in the formulas in the dictionary, but which is defined in their use together; gesture is that meaningfulness which is moving, in every sense of that word; what moves the words and what moves us." Gesture is "made of the language beneath or beyond or alongside of the language of words." Gesture must be "carried into [language] whenever the context is imaginative." Having defined gesture in poetry, Blackmur addresses himself to two questions: how is gesture expressed in language, and how may gesture be accounted for in the critical act? Blackmur's answer is that gesture is expressed through the forms of language and may be accounted for in the critical act through analysis of these forms, or structures.

The simplest structural form that may embody gesture is repetition. Blackmur cites Macbeth's "Tomorrow and tomorrow and tomorrow," and Lear's "never, never, never, never, never," as "immediate examples of simple repetition metamorphosing the most familiar words into the most engulfing meaning"; and, Blackmur states, "It is not at all the meaning the words *had* that counts, but the meaning that repetition, in a given situation, makes them take on." Iago's "Put money in thy purse" speech to Roderigo is a more complex kind of repetition than the syllabic repetitions of Lear and Macbeth. Repeated throughout Iago's speech, the immediate meaning of the phrase is subordinated to the meanings *it takes on,* Blackmur says, as a result of the repetition. The phrase becomes indicative of the change in Roderigo and indicative also of Iago's evil. In short, the phrase becomes gesture. While the rest of Iago's speech could have been changed, Blackmur believes that Iago's "Put money in thy purse" could not be altered "without altering the gesture."

In Hamlet's soliloquy "it is the context that determines the meaningfulness that the words *die* and *sleep* and their variant take on in the process of becoming gesture." When the words have become gesture, what they express is all "the ill of doubt and trepidation before the unknown prospect which the words 'to die: to sleep' release as gesture, which in turn infect the triple, mutilating repetition [to Ophelia's question:] 'Well, well, well.' "

Another kind of repetition that is controlled by the context is Macbeth's speech "Sleep no more / Macbeth does murder sleep!" In this example of gesture in language, Blackmur says, the repetition of "sleep" comes only at the beginning of the passage "and is only implied, in the played upon sense, through the rest of the passage." Blackmur means that not only is the ordinary meaning of the word "sleep" submerged in favor of its cumulus of associations, but the meaning itself is "detached" from the word and made the subject of the passage by the rest of the context. The word "sleep" after its initial repetitions, is no longer necessary to the rest of the passage because its cumulus of associations creates "other gestures in the last four phrases, which themselves both play upon each other and all backwards upon sleep." The two passages from *Hamlet* and *Macbeth* have in common the "power of discovered or invoked gesture to transform the simple name of sleep into a rich and complex symbol."

Punning is another way of expressing gesture in language. The poet begins with the ordinary meaning of a word and contrasts it with its other possible meanings, thereby creating "tension" among the various meanings. And this tension expresses gesture. Further, Blackmur says, the pun

taken in its fullest gamut as gesture (for any achieved pun is a gesture), [is] the only direct avenue to undifferentiated sense that a poet has; it is what objectively joins the perceptions of the different senses together, heightening them into a single sensation. Not only that, but it also—and this is our chosen nexus—produces an undifferentiated gesture of meaning; under masterly hands punning is the onomatopoeia of meaning. Which is to say that the play upon words is both the most immediate and most final congeries of signs; it is the very gesture which identifies the elements of the sound with the elements of meaning.

The pun, then, is the only "direct avenue" whereby the world of gesture may be objectively expressed in language. At the most basic level, the pun translates the quality of sound into something quantitative which may be measured by the critic. Blackmur takes three more examples from William Shakespeare to illustrate.

The first example is the word "vast" as used in the phrase, "In the dead vast and middle of the night" spoken by Horatio to Hamlet. In various printings, Blackmur explains, the word has been printed as "vast," "wast," and "waste." The various meanings that each of these words have, says Blackmur, do not change the overall meaning of the phrase because "no matter which way the word is printed the effect of all three is evident and felt, with a strong possibility of a fourth sense, that of *waist*, as well. The accident of the recorded variations in printing forces the attention upon the variety of meanings bedded down to sleep in this single syllable." And, Blackmur continues,

Let us read the line in the middle spelling: "In the dead wast and middle of the night," and do we not have all at once in the word the sense of the vast void of the night, the stretching and useless waste of the night, and the waist or middle and generative part of the night as well? And do we not have, finally, a kind of undifferentiated meaning which is a product of all three, a gesture of meaning which can only be less defined the more deeply it is experienced?

The undifferentiated meaning, the gesture, is not only more important than the individual meanings of these words, but in Blackmur's view it is what Shakespeare meant to express. Blackmur's second example from Shakespeare points this out more clearly. "There is a line in Macbeth," he says, "when murder is all acanter in the offing, which images 'in his surcease, success.'" There is almost a direct contradiction in the literal meaning of the two most important words, "yet in the gesture or play which the two make together there is a new meaningfulness that could not be produced without the play." And Blackmur contends that it is this "new" meaningfulness created by the context of the play that Shakespeare meant to express.

The third example is from Sonnet 129. Blackmur quotes the lines: "Past reason hunted, and no sooner had, / Past reason hated." The interplay, he says, between "hunted" and "hated" gives rise to the gesture expressed by "haunted"; for, Blackmur says, "Surely one is haunted by what one both hunts and hates."

Generalizing from these three examples, Blackmur reaches several conclusions concerning gesture. First, words tend to become gesture when they are "momentarily deprived of their normal meanings." Second, gesture "constitutes the revelation of the *sum* or *product* of all the meanings possible within the focus of the words played upon." And third, in poetry at least, the words "transformed into gesture . . . carry the load, wield the load, lighten the load, and leap beyond the load of meaning."

Gesture, then, may be expressed through various poetic and artistic techniques which have the effect of momentarily suspending the literal meanings of words. In Blackmur's opinion, Wallace Stevens is the eminent manipulator of words into gesture; but he is only one, Blackmur says, among a whole generation of poets who have consciously attempted such manipulation. "The whole movement in the arts known progressively as dadaism and surrealism was devoted, in its poetry," Blackmur continues, "to releasing such gestures from language by the deliberate obliteration of the normal modes of meaning from the context."

In the critical act, gesture may be accounted for by "mooring" (Blackmur's term) it to "such formal agents as plot and meter and refrain." Again, Blackmur is following other New Critics here in seeking value in the technical or formal elements of the poem. How gesture may be moored to plot is "too large an order to discuss in the limited space of an essay," Blackmur says, but he does say that "it is the stress and urgency of plot that determine *what* gestures are wanted and by its exigencies *when* they shall be released." Meter and refrain are easier to handle.

Taking Coleridge's definition that meter is the motion of meaning, Blackmur turns it around to say that "motion is the meter of meaning." That is, "if meter as motion brings meaning to gesture, then motion as meter moors gesture to meaning. There is a mutual tying down process, in the operation of meter, a strict and precise delivery of detail in an order of movement, which, well used, gives a sense of absolute speed and absolute position otherwise unavailable to the poet." Refrain gives a "particular form, on a general and dependable model to gesture that might otherwise be formless." "Refrain is the emphatic measure of all those gestures that have to do with the declaration of recurrence, return, rebirth and new birth, of motion in stillness and stillness in motion, of permanence in change, and change in permanence. It is the lyric gesture of recognition and emphatic gesture of identity." Gesture, then, in the critical act, is accounted for through an analysis of the formal or technical aspects of the poem and, by extension, through the formal elements of any work of art. And the presence of gesture is determined by the critic's imagination.

Working from the statements Blackmur makes in the two essays just reviewed, it is possible to reach some conclusions concerning his critical canon. Blackmur's general critical goal is to establish criticism on a base of unimpeachable rationality. He wants to establish a critical method that will guarantee scientific rigor, yet at the same time he is not seeking critical conclusions that would be universally valid. To understand this apparent paradox in his thought, it is necessary to understand how he views or sees, finally, the two fundamental elements of his criticism—the critical object and the critical process.

To Blackmur, the critical object has a viable and verifiable spiritual as well as temporal reality. The facts of a work indicate its spatio-temporal or "real" existence while gesture indicates its spiritual existence. As we have just seen, gesture is not something tangible that can be objectively proven to exist; it is something intangible that may only be asserted to exist. Gesture is felt or intuited psychically just as one can sometimes intuit which horse will win before a race. That part of the mind which deals with these psychological predilections, in Blackmur's scheme, is the imagination. That part of the mind which deals with the facts of a work is called reason.

Since a work of art exists on two levels, the critical act is not complete unless it takes both levels into account. In terms of the critical act, the two levels are interdependent; that is, gesture is embedded or "moored" in the facts of a work. The focal point of Blackmur's criticism is *inside* the phenomenon or critical object itself. To establish the focal point of criticism it is necessary to analyze first the object as it exists in the real world. In Blackmur's description of the critical act, the critic begins with an analysis of the facts of the work. Facts are the materials of the work—its medium and the way the medium is utilized. Only when the critic begins with the facts of the work can he arrive at a point in the critical act where he can intuit the essence of the work which lies on the spiritual level of the critical object's dual existence. These are the assumptions that Blackmur makes about the nature of the art work and about the nature of the critical act.

The next general comment that might be made concerns evaluation. Obviously, if critical evaluation depended solely upon the facts of a work there would be no problem. Other critics could verify Blackmur's evaluations simply by referring to the critical object. In other words, it could be investigated empirically. But to Blackmur the critical process is a two-step process involving the critical object on its two levels of reality. Critical evaluation depends on not only an analysis of the facts but also on an intuitive or imaginative accounting of the psychical aspects of the critical object. This imaginative dimension of the critical act, however, creates the problem of normative evaluation. If normative evaluation is to be possible in Blackmur's criticism, there must be some criteria by which his imaginative accounting of the spiritual aspects of the critical object can be checked. And, obviously, these criteria must be themselves outside of the spiritual realm; that is, they must lie in the realm of reason so that they may be used as a means of verifying or correlating critical judgments. And Blackmur does use criteria in the realm of reason when he uses the external criteria of rhyme, meter, repetition, and so forth as a normative check on his imagination. Evaluation is possible, then, in his criticism because the imaginative or spiritual dimension is "anchored" to the analytical dimension. In other words, the facts of the critical object circumscribe the limits of imagination.

But now another question arises. If evaluation is possible, then how in his system can Blackmur account for the vast variety of differences in critical judgment? That is, why do critics arrive at such different judgments given the same facts? Blackmur partly answers this question in "A Critic's Job of Work" by saying that not all the facts of a work are available to any one critic. But his answer is insufficient and needs expanding. While it is true that not all critics will "see" the same facts because their critical methods are predisposed to discover one kind of fact over another, there is a more satisfactory explanation for the question of critical diversity, and one that is implicit in Blackmur's thought. To explain, I must introduce an idea found in his "A Burden for Critics." "The institution of literature," he writes, "so far as it is alive, is made again at every instant. It is made afresh as part of the process of being known afresh; what is permanent is what is always fresh, and it can be fresh only in performance — that is, in reading and seeing and hearing what is actually in it at this place and this time."[4] The key to an understanding of evaluative diversity derived from Blackmur's thought lies in his idea that the institution of literature is renewed relative to its historical position. If the institution of literature is reduced here to a single work for ease in handling, the question may then be put, "What is it about this work that is permanent yet always fresh, relative to its historical position?" There are three possible answers. If, as Blackmur believes, the work can be divided into what may be empirically known through the critic's reason and into what may be intuitively known through the critic's imagination, then what is permanent yet fresh about this work can either be its facts (compositional techniques), its gesture embodied in the facts, or a combination of both. The first and third possibilities are not satisfactory because the facts of a work, by themselves or in combination with gesture may not be fresh even though they are a permanent part of the work. Once introduced, the compositional techniques of prose and of poetry can hardly appear fresh in an historical perspective. Even a work like Joyce's *Ulysses*, as far as compositional techniques go, can be seen as an imitation of *Tristram Shandy*. This leaves the second possibility that what is permanent yet fresh in a work is its gesture; or, that quality in the work that can be only perceived imaginatively.

Gesture is a part of the work just as facts are, yet it is continually fresh because it must be continually recaptured imaginatively by different critics at different points of time and of place. While gesture is a permanent part of the work, its apprehension is historically relative. If the critical act must include the imaginative apprehension of gesture which is relative to the time and place of the critic, then this relativity can also account for the diversity of critical opinion. This explanation introduces another idea important in Blackmur's critical canon. There exists, he believes, a dynamic relationship between critics and literature which he calls "performance." Because the imaginative recapturing of gesture is historically relative "The job of putting the audience into relation to the work of art not only has to be done over again, which is to the good and a sign of vitality, but the job is often so difficult that we cannot do it ourselves, there being something lacking in our dominant methods, and we are compelled to rehearse an old job of work done in a different language in a different situation to a different tune."[5] The critic's job may be difficult but it is certain that it must be done over and over again. If the critic could make a judgment about a work that would be valid for all time there would be no need for continual revaluations. But this is Blackmur's point: because the imaginative recapturing of gesture is historically relative, there can be no absolute in critical evaluation even though the critical process itself can aspire to emulate the empirical method of science.

III   *The Social Role of the Critic*

To Blackmur, critical judgment is also a social act and involves the critic in analyses of social conditions. Blackmur's fundamental insight into twentieth-century social conditions is that both artists and audiences have lost their ability to make their human experience meaningful. In Blackmur's view, to be covered more fully later, artists and audiences no longer respond to their experience with reason and imagination and are therefore unable to make any sense of their experience. Given these social conditions Blackmur sees the role of the critic as that of a mediator between society and the arts. Blackmur believes that the relationship between society and art is symbiotic; art expresses or reflects society and society is the source of material for art. Judgment of art in this view is also judgment of society. Since the critic is himself part of society—and in order that he may understand his own social experience—he must respond to his society with the same critical tools he uses in critiquing. artworks. In Blackmur's terminology the critic responds to his society with reason and imagination.

I would like to turn now to a consideration of Blackmur's conception of the mediating role of the critic and how he thinks the critic may best respond to his own social experience. I will begin with a reading of Blackmur's essay "A Featherbed for Critics," in which is explained the relationship of the critic to the artist. I will next consider "A Burden for Critics," where Blackmur delineates the relationship of the critic to society. And last, from "The Lion and the Honeycomb," I will try to draw out how the critic should respond to his social experience and what his criteria for judging the arts on a social scale should be.

IV   *"A Featherbed for Critics"*

"A Featherbed for Critics" was written in 1940 and is an example of Blackmur's increasing concentration on social themes.[6] His intent in this essay is "frankly hortatory, tactlessly moral; and it is undertaken because of those feelings, in a rising gorge, of stress, unease, and perfidious futility which form the base of immediate reaction to the general impact of writing in America." In this passage Blackmur is alluding to what he considers is the insufficient response of American society to her writers. Leaving aside for the moment what an insufficient response is, Blackmur is more concerned with what the critic can do for writers and all artists who lack a spiritually sustaining and nourishing response from their societies.

The role of the critic, he says, is "to lead writers where they are necessarily going" and "to bring them to a full consciousness of their profession . . . to situate the profession in society." To lead writers where they are going means that the critic must help the writer "to envisage under what conditions, toward what nearly impossible ambition, he had best move to secure the maximum responsibility [to society] in his work." Blackmur means that the critic must aid the writer in understanding what he must do to make the experience he writes about meaningful to himself and to society. The critic must first remind the writer to "keep himself in a steady startled state: as if one were about to be haunted; as if one were never to get used to, and hence never to let down, one's powers of vision, one's resources of feeling." The critic must also make sure that the writer realizes that in selecting the experience he wishes to communicate he must perform *"the most arduous critical act of which he is capable."* "It is in this sense," Blackmur writes, "that the composition of a great poem is a labor of unrelenting criticism, and the full reading of it only less so; and it is in this sense, too, that the critical act is what is called a 'creative' act, whether [it is performed] by poet, critic, or serious reader, since there is an alternative, a stretching, of the sensibility as the act is done." The writer selects his experience to communicate in accordance with his view or attitude of life that Blackmur calls in this essay "conviction."

A writer's conviction, Blackmur says, is his "inward mastery of the outward materials of experience," and that "final human feeling towards experience." It is conviction that *"alone gives a writer objective authority in his work."* Further, Blackmur believes, "in the first society of the western world not based upon the religious imagination . . . the critic must give to the writer 'the bread and wine of conviction.'" Blackmur does not say precisely how the critic would be able to give conviction, but he believes that after having studied the works of a particular writer, the critic could then discover the latent convictions or attitude to life manifested in the work and make these convictions known to the writer himself. Blackmur assumes that most writers write without convictions, or at least do not consciously know what their convictions are. He believes that modern writers have this problem because they do not have an institutional source of beliefs like the Church and hence have difficulty in identifying convictions derived from within themselves but which do not have any institutional sanction.

Bringing writers "to a full consciousness of their profession" means that the critic must act as a kind of Arnoldian historian of the best that has been thought and said. The critic educates writers in the tradition and institution of letters. He should make them aware, Blackmur says, that they are not writing "alone, or anyhow willfully, but together with many as the product of the tension of a lifetime, his own life seen in the life of his society." The critic "must secure and elevate the profession, to save and improve the professional habit of the whole possible band of serious writers, from which the individual appears and without which he cannot survive his apparition even the meagre remnant of his lifetime."

The critic must also "situate the profession [of writing] in society." "For," Blackmur says, "there is a profession of society, and there is a sense, here hoped for as present, in which the profession of society and the profession of writing are the same." Both the writer and his society are seeking meaning. This quest should be reflected in the writer's work and in society's demand for "high level" or meaningful writing. Unfortunately, Blackmur continues, there is no such demand, and without the demand, high-level writing has not flourished. "We might put it," he says, "that the demand together with the capacity for informed seriousness in high level popular novels has fallen off. Again, it could rather be said that the demand and capacity for fact, excitement, urgency have overwhelmed the high seriousness that might otherwise have fostered good writing." In addition to not demanding of its writers high-level writing, society even tries to seduce writers away from the profession of writing by offering well-paid teaching, lecturing, editing, or publishing jobs. The result is that what may have been otherwise serious literature has become vitiated into something else. *"Grapes of Wrath* and *Native Son* are perhaps as far as we can profitably go," he says, "in the direction of serious writing, and it is no accident that the first has been compared with *Uncle Tom's Cabin* and the second has been so widely accepted as a document."

It is the responsibility of the critic, as the man in the middle, to remind writers of the need for high-level writing, and, through criticism, to create a new appreciation for it. Between writers and all artists and their societies "a deep collaboration is necessary, a collaboration in which the forces are autonomous and may never consciously cooperate, but which is marked by the unity they make together and by the culture which the individual, by the art of his convicted imagination, brings to light."

V   *"A Burden for Critics"*

In this essay Blackmur uses three terms that are important to an understanding of the critic's responsibilities. These three terms are "momentum," "performance," and "aesthetic." Blackmur pictures society as a dynamic continuum, and the word he uses to describe that state is "momentum." All things that are part of society—the artist, the arts, the critic, the people, and their collective beliefs—are in momentum. While all the elements of society are moving, they are also shifting and changing in relationship to each other. For instance, the relationship of a particular belief to an artist or critic or to any other member of society may change. Similarly, the relationship of critics to artists, or to society in general, may change. But at this time and in this place, Blackmur says, the relationship between society and the arts has so shifted that the burden of criticism in our time is "to make bridges between the society and the arts: to prepare the audience for its art and to prepare the arts for their artists."

The building of these bridges is called "performance." Performance is a new term adopted by Blackmur to describe the critical act. He introduces this term to underscore his belief that the critical act is a dynamic act and that the institution of literature "is made afresh as part of the process of being known afresh; what is permanent is what is always fresh, and it can be fresh only in performance—that is, in reading and seeing and hearing what is actually in it at this time and this place." In Blackmur's view, the critic establishes the relationships among the individual work, the artist, and society, through the critical act (performance). Taking just the creative work and the audience, Blackmur states that "performance, the condition we are after, cannot mean the same thing to the audience and the artist. The audience needs instruction in the lost skill of symbolic thinking. The arts need rather to be shown how their old roles can be played in new conditions. To do either, both need to be allied to the intellectual habits of the time." The role the critic must play in society is the role of instructor in symbolic thinking. Through the critical act the critic must establish the meaning of the symbols used in any work because the general audience has lost the ability to do so. But merely establishing the meaning of symbols is not enough. "Besides analysis, elucidation, and comparison," Blackmur says, "which Eliot once listed as the functions of criticism, criticism in our time must also come to judgment." To judge, the critic must have some standard, and at this point in his essay Blackmur introduces the term "aesthetic." "I see no reason why all forms of the word *aesthetic* cannot be restored to good society among literary critics by remembering its origin in a Greek word meaning to perceive, and remembering also its gradual historical limitation to what is perceived or felt—that is, what is actually there—in the arts." The critic's standard for judgment is an aesthetic standard. To Blackmur,

aesthetics comprises the study of superficial and mechanical executive techniques, partly in themselves, but also and mainly in relation to the ulterior techniques of conceptual form and of symbolic form. . . . The main study of executive techniques will always be, to repeat, in relation to the ulterior techniques of conceptual and symbolic form. By conceptual techniques I mean the rationale of what the artist does with his dominant convictions, or obsessions, or insights, or visions, and how they are translated into major stresses of human relation as they are actually experienced. . . . By symbolic techniques I mean what happens in the arts—*what gets into the arts*—that makes them relatively inexhaustible so long as they are understood.

From this statement three elements in Blackmur's aesthetic standard can be determined. One, the study of executive techniques or the form of the work, must always be seen in relation to the second, the ulterior techniques of conceptual form, or content of the work. This is another formulation of Blackmur's idea expressed previously that a work consists of facts (executive techniques) and gesture (symbolic techniques), both of which are determined by the third element of

Blackmur's aesthetic—the artist's attitude or point of view concerning his experience.

Blackmur bases his critical judgments on these three elements, which comprise his aesthetic standard. However,

Because the arts are imperfect, they can be judged only imperfectly by aesthetic means. They must be judged, therefore, by the declaration and elucidation of identity in terms of the whole enterprise which they feed, and of which they are the play, the aesthetic experience. There is a confusion here that cannot be clarified for it is a confusion of real things, as words are confused in a line of verse, the better the line the more completely, so that we cannot tell which ones govern the others. The confusion is, that it is through the aesthetic experience of it that we discover, and discover again, what life is, and that at present, if our account of it is correct, we also discover what our culture is.

Blackmur means that the arts are the artists' aesthetic experience of their culture; and to judge the arts, the critic must himself work through his own aesthetic experience of his culture. This is the confusion that Blackmur refers to because, in effect, the critic judges one aesthetic experience by another. To be sure, the critic also judges the work through its executive techniques, but he judges these techniques in relation to the artists' and to his own aesthetic experience of culture.

VI   *"The Lion and the Honeycomb"*

In this essay, Blackmur introduces the concept of the "scholar-critic" who "must be the master-layman of as many modes of human understanding as is possible in a single mind."[7] Twenty years earlier in "A Critic's Job of Work" Blackmur had stated that one of the first jobs of the critic was the job of scholarship or the collection of facts. But scholarship, he said, did not go far enough—it collected the facts but did not explain their connection to the mystery of life. In this essay he combines two jobs, the collection of facts and the deciphering of mysteries, in one man.

"I say a master-layman," Blackmur begins, "because he is committed not to the creation of experience, but to the response to experience no matter how far short of direct knowledge of the experience his sensibility might come; and I say a master-layman, too, because this ideal monster, the complete scholar-critic, as such, cannot permit himself properly the extravagant delight (though he may unawares fall into it) of making his response by means of any single method or mode of the mind exlusively." The essential points in this passage are that the scholar-critic is committed to making a response to experience and that the response cannot be made by any single method or mode of mind. In Blackmur's view, the critic is by definition someone who responds to experience. To judge the arts, Blackmur has said, the critic must work through his own aesthetic experience of his society and culture. In this particular essay Blackmur states explicitly that "criticism deals with the experience of the ideas (or feelings, or what not) *in* the work." And the critic is committed to respond to this experience in the work. He cannot respond, Blackmur says, by means of any single method or mode of mind exclusively. That the critic should not use any single critical method exclusively is understandable because any exclusive use of one method, Blackmur has cautioned, would lead to unwarranted distortions in meaning.

Continuing in the essay, Blackmur equates scholarship with reason and criticism with imagination. "Scholarship is *about* literature, describes it, surrounds it, identifies its content, and supplies what is lacking because of the movement of time or the shift in the conventions of the literary mind." Scholarship is that part of the critical act which discovers the facts about a work, or scholarship is another name for what reason does in the critical act. Criticism, in this formulation by Blackmur, since it deals with the experience that is in literature, corresponds to that part of the critical act which is imaginative. "Criticism," he writes, "accords to the act of imitation or creation. . . . Criticism is within, scholarship without, the work." When criticism and scholarship "edge into each other," Blackmur says, "in the limbo between is that extraordinarily complicated thing called full appreciation short of judgment; for appreciation with judgment requires the ultimately simple act of scholarship and criticism combined in a single intuition." The ideal combination of scholarship and criticism would result from combining Aristotle's method with that of Samuel Taylor Coleridge.

Coleridge began the whole business of the special techniques of modern scholarship and criticism of poetry; all the expansions into the psychology of language and imagination. Aristotle is there to absorb and unite the excesses of these techniques in the terms and under the force of my analogy; the force and illumination of the joint presence of poetic, dialectic, and rhetoric. . . . By poetic is meant: the creative action of the mind which has an eye to truth in the objects it makes. Dialectic has nothing to do with Hegel. By dialectic is meant: the reasonable conversation of the mind which has an eye to truth in ideas. By rhetoric is meant: the art of persuasion, properly, in the service of dialectic or poetic.

This is another, subtler formulation of the role of the critic and his relationship to the artwork. *Poetic* means imaginative perception of truth to experience that Blackmur has been saying is one of the essential criteria of the aesthetic experience. *Dialectic* means creation of order out of the chaos of experience and *rhetoric* alludes to the social requirement of the critic to persuade and convince artists and audiences that belief and conviction is possible.

The five essays considered in this chapter were written over a period of twenty years, from 1935 to 1955. They reflect occasional needs and interests and also the increasing complexity of Blackmur's thought on the nature and responsibilities of criticism. From seeing the work as a separate, self-contained entity, and the function of the critic being solely to discover the meaning of the work, Blackmur's thought evolves to his seeing the work as a point in a social nexus and the critic's job as being to rationalize and to explain the connections between the work and the artist, the audience, and society. Of course, even in his later formulations Blackmur believed that the critic had to determine the meaning of the work; but his emphasis in his later writings centers on the critic as a builder of bridges between art and its audience and their society.

From the very start of his career to its latest point, Blackmur held remarkably clear and consistent ideas that tended to be expressed more poetically as he grew older. The subtle formulations of his basic concepts that occur in his later work have tended to obscure those ideas and made some critics overreact to such Blackmurian notions as combining Aristotle with Coleridge. When he makes such suggestions, it must be remembered from his very first essay on the critical process that he said a critic should borrow whatever he needs from wherever he can, leaving out the logical difficulties associated with terminologies and doctrines. It must be remembered also that Blackmur believed that the critic recreated the conditions that led to the creation of the work under review. Therefore, in a very literal sense, criticism to Blackmur was a creative act, and, as such, was likely to reach out for and include impressions and images in the mind of the critic. In this way, Blackmur combined Aristotle with Coleridge because they represented two impressions in his mind of generally different ways of perceiving the artwork. I don't mean to imply unclear or mistaken reasoning on Blackmur's part; rather, I mean to imply poetic thinking and linking of what appeared to him to be linkable things.

To reiterate, Blackmur's ideas on the critic's job and on the nature of the art object are simple and consistently held throughout his long career. Because the work of art has a dual nature, the critic's job must be twofold. It is interesting to note that duality is pervasive in Blackmur's criticism and it is interesting also to speculate that, as a poet writing criticism, Blackmur must have keenly felt the duality in his own nature. In fact, it might be said that his perception of duality is his fundamental critical insight. The work of art has a form and it has a content, and the critic must examine both. The form can be examined reasonably because it is *there* for all to see. The content cannot be analyzed in the same way because it is too amorphous, too relative to individual perception to be handled any way but imaginatively by the critic. These are not new and original ideas with Blackmur, nor is the thrust of his criticism to combine the critical handling of form and content (executive techniques and gesture) in some systematic way new. In this he was led by the New Critics. Even his ideas on the social role of the critic are not new. In this he was preceded by many, including Matthew Arnold, Henry James, and T. S. Eliot. What is new and different in his critical thought is his attempt to combine, or, I should say, reintegrate the dualities he perceived into unities or fusions of sensibility. If he perceived the artwork as having a dual nature, he nevertheless wanted to discover a way in which the two halves could be made into a unity where form grew out of content and content grew out of form. If the artist and the critic had a dual nature, then Blackmur wanted to show how a unified sensibility could be manufactured through the agency of artistic creation. And, finally, if society had, in his view, leaned too heavily on a materialistic and mechanistic view of life in opposition to or in reaction against an idealistic and spiritual view of life, then, he believed, it was the role of the critic to discover or rediscover the way to fuse in harmony the spiritual with the material. This, of course, was and is a colossal undertaking for a critic. Those with less sympathy for Blackmur's purposes might supply other, less flattering adjectives to his motives, but the idea of it, the fact that he seems to have set this undertaking out as a critical goal, gives an insight, I think, into why he had such an affinity for Henry Adams.

CHAPTER 4

Blackmur and Henry Adams

BLACKMUR shared with Henry Adams a private belief wherein the highest good was to seek a harmony that was both personally and universally valid. They were both moralists and critics of Western culture, and both took as their primary artistic task the discovery of an aesthetic form that would serve the expression of their perceptions of Western culture.

Blackmur received a Guggenheim grant in 1937 to begin work on a critical biography of Adams. Although he published several essays from the work in progress, Blackmur never finished the project (see Chronology). Perhaps because as a critic he was more interested in the problems of aesthetic form, Blackmur found himself unable to concentrate on the realities of Henry Adams, the man. All Blackmur's published essays on Adams concentrate on Adams's artistic problems, particularly on the problem of finding a satisfactory form for perceptions that were for Adams, and for Blackmur also, partly imaginative, partly historical, and partly unconscious.

Blackmur follows Adams's search for a satisfactory aesthetic form through two novels, through *The Education,* and through *Mont-Saint-Michel and Chartres.* Interestingly, Blackmur views this search objectively yet with great sympathy for Adams's artistic frustration and ultimate failure. Adams was, for Blackmur, a great man in the sense of greatness as a measure of one's refusal to accept less than one's goal. This "scrupulosity" was the real link between Blackmur and Adams as brothers in art. This chapter focuses attention on Blackmur's interest in Adams's search for an aesthetic form appropriate to cultural criticism.

I Henry Adams

Henry Brooks Adams (1838–1918) was the grandson of John Quincy Adams, sixth president of the United States. As a member of one of America's most prominent political and social families, Adams had a heritage of leadership and action, but by his own account he was reticent and shy with a love of literature that set him apart from the family norm. After his graduation from Harvard, he successively became a journalist, editor, professor, historian, and artist. Each one of these successions was accompanied by a corresponding change in depth of feeling and understanding of himself as he sought to understand the universe through himself. In the two books by which he is best remembered, *Mont-Saint-Michel and Chartres* and *The Education of Henry Adams,* he finally discovered a form for an intense and imaginative rendering of his experience.

What was Adams's experience for which he felt the need for imaginative artistic expression? As a man of the nineteenth century, alive at a time of accelerating economic, social, and philosophical change, his fundamental insight was into the divisive forces at work spiritually and materially on man. In his view, man was incapable of controlling his own destiny or shaping outside of himself the course of events. His determination to explain how this state of affairs had come about led to ever more creative, imaginative works—works in which he sought to discover for himself and for his age—a point of view, a meaningful unity in the divisive forces loose in the universe.

By "force" Adams meant an impersonal-personal, unconscious-conscious phenomenon that manifested itself in the history of the world. Examples of force were slavery, civil law. religion, evolution, the compass, greek fire, in short, any idea, discovery, social development, or tool that effected a change in man's conception of himself. In the chapter "A Dynamic Theory of History," from *The Education,* Adams pictured man as a force surrounded by and acted upon by other forces in constant, continual motion much as Blackmur pictured the critic in momentum. "The universe that had formed [man]," Adams wrote,

took shape in his mind as a reflection of his own unity, containing all forces except himself. Either separately, or in groups, or as a whole, these forces never ceased to act on him, enlarging his mind as they enlarged the surface foliage of a vegetable, and the mind needed only to respond, as the forest did, to these attractions. Susceptibility to highest forces is the highest genius; selection between them is the highest science; their mass is the highest educator.[1]

To Adams, the history of man was the history of man's response
to forces which opened his mind to knowledge; his accumulation
of knowledge which allowed him to explain and to manipulate
Nature; and the collision and diversion of forces which taught
painful lessons. The motive that set the dynamic in motion was
man's "appetite for power." "Man's function as a force of nature
was to assimilate other forces as he assimilated food. He called it
the love of power. He felt his own feebleness, and he sought for
an ass or a camel, a bow or a sling, to widen his range of power, as
he sought a fetish or a planet in the world beyond."[2] Man
symbolized as *unity*, Adams said, the whole phenomena of forces
acting upon him, including himself, and worshiped it as God. But,
he continued, "Except as reflected in himself, man has no reason
for assuming unity in the universe, or an ultimate substance, or a
prime motor. The *a priori* insistence on this unity ended by
fatiguing the more active—or reactive—minds; and Lord Bacon
tried to stop it. He urged society to lay aside the idea of evolving
the universe from a thought, and to try evolving thought from
the universe."[3] In other words, man should stop trying to give
meaning to the universe with ideas such as *unity* and start
deriving meaning from his perceptions of the universe. From
1500 onward, Adams said, new discoveries in science and trade
began to effect a change in man's attitude about himself. His
power to control and to manipulate Nature through ideas
became increasingly useless, and with the decline in power came
a questioning of potency. "The microscope," Adams wrote,
"revealed a universe that defied the senses; gunpowder killed
whole races that lagged behind; the compass coerced the most
imbruted mariner to act on the impossible idea that the earth
was round; the press drenched Europe with anarchism. Europe
saw itself, violently resisting, wrenched into false positions,
drawn along new lines as a fish that is caught on a hook; but
unable to understand by what force it was controlled."[4] Man
began to depend upon his instruments rather than upon his
perception and the force of science became stronger as the
momentum of discoveries accelerated. Finally, by 1900,

Science has proved that forces, sensible and occult, physical and
metaphysical, simple and complex, surround, traverse, vibrate, rotate,
repel, attract, without stop; that man's senses are conscious of few, and
only in a partial degree; but that, from the beginning of organic

existence his consciousness has been induced, expanded, trained in the lines of his sensitiveness; and that the rise of his faculties from a lower power to a higher, or from a narrower to a wider field, may be due to the function of assimilating and storing outside force or forces. There is nothing unscientific in the idea that, beyond the lines of force felt by the senses, the universe may be—as it has always been—either a supersensuous chaos or a divine unity, which irresistibly attracts, and is either life or death to penetrate.[5]

What, then, in Adams's view, was man's present metaphysical situation? Surrounded and acted upon by multiple forces, chief among them those of science and the scientific method, could man ever find meaning again in his experience? To answer this question became Adams's spiritual quest. First, as he himself said, he had to find a unit of measurement. By what yardstick could meaning be measured? And, after that, what formula would solve the equation of human history?

The yardstick he found, as he pointed out in "The Abyss of Ignorance" chapter in *The Education,* was "the point of history when man held the highest idea of himself as a unit in a unified universe . . . the century 1150–1250, expressed in Amiens Cathedral and the Works of Thomas Aquinas . . . the unit [by] which he might measure motion [human destiny] down to his own time, without assuming anything as true or untrue, except relation." In this century, Adams believed, man had reached the peak of his development because he had succeeded through the agency of the Church, in attaining a unity or equilibrium of forces. The unity was achieved by an act of inner psychological force which by tradition he called God. This idea of unity—this assertion of will—became Adams's measuring unit. And measured in this way, the history of man since the twelfth century was a history of the progressive loss of will or unity and a corresponding rise in the power of other forces, particularly those of science, to shape man's world. Instead of unity, man's world in the nineteenth and twentieth centuries was one of multiplicity governed by the scientific method. The formula Adams adopted for human history was the second law of thermodynamics, the law of dissipation of energy. All energy dissipates equally in a closed system so that human energy, Adams reasoned, had dissipated from its highest concentration in twelfth-century Europe to its present low level, but new

energies, new forces, were in the offing and these new forces
came under the heading of science.

As an artist, Adams tried to express these new forces by using
science as an instrument of the imagination rather than as an
instrument for the gathering of facts. In the most famous chapter
in *The Education,* "The Dynamo and the Virgin," Adams
recounted his efforts to discover a symbol of science that would
have the same transcendental power as did the symbol of the
Virgin in the twelfth century. "Symbol or energy, the Virgin had
acted as the greatest force the Western world ever felt, and had
drawn man's activities to herself more strongly than any other
power, natural or supernatural, had ever done. . . . All the
steam in the world could not, like the Virgin, build Chartres." To
find such a symbol for the twentieth century was Adams's artistic
problem and the point of interest to Blackmur. Adams represented to Blackmur the quintessential artist-critic who created
the interpretation of his age in an imaginative critical work.

II   *Blackmur's Study of Adams*

In his best essay on Adams Blackmur wrote:

In Adams the attractive force is in the immediate relevance that his life
and works have for our own. The problems he posed of human energy
and human society are felt at once to be special and emphatic
articulations of our own problems. The disseminative, central force,
which we find objectified in his works, may be felt and seen as the
incandescence of the open, enquiring, sensitive, and sceptical intelligence, restless but attentive, saltatory but serial, provisional in every
position yet fixed upon a theme: the theme of thought or imagination
conceived as the form of human energy.[6]

This statement could apply equally as well to Blackmur himself.
The problems he and Adams chose to face are problems of the
human spirit in conflict with human culture. And they both faced
these problems with the same kind of intelligence and with the
same theme.

Adams spent his adult life, Blackmur writes, searching for the
unifying meaning of his experience. Adams felt that his personal
experience was representative of his age, so that in discovering
the meaning of his own experience he would at the same time

discover the meaning of the collective experience of his generation. Adams's generation, Blackmur continues, faced the peculiar dilemma expressed in Matthew Arnold's lines: "Wandering between two worlds, one dead / The other powerless to be born." Adams was old enough to have spent his childhood and adolescence in the years before the Civil War. To his generation, the years following the war seemed to be palpably different, materially and spiritually, from anything they had known previously.

In the year 1858, Henry Adams graduated from Harvard College. In 1859 appeared Darwin's *Origin of Species.* Thermodynamics, Accounting, Electromagnetism, Political Realism, and the Corporation were new institutions—or new forms of old institutions—drawing energy and materialistic bias from the new studies. Political Europe—and European Culture—expanded in scope and speed and fragmented both internally and externally because it was not able to maintain unity in the interests of its new intensities. . . . What had happened . . . was that man had been put into possession of vast stores of new energy which as he learned to use them carried him away, and which his intelligence could neither keep up nor cope with.[7]

The cultural forces accelerated and created by the Civil War were beyond Adams's and his generation's intellectual capacity to control. These new forces had upset their feeling of spiritual unity, inducing in them a psychological uneasiness—a malaise of the spirit. To a generation whose youth lay on the other side of a devastating war, the cultural responses formed before the war were inadequate to their new experience. The task of Adams's generation, then, was to reorient themselves and find a new meaning for their experience.

The task was not easy. In the first place, Blackmur writes

What seemed to have disappeared was the means to express human reaction and aspiration in terms of great symbols. The disappearance was of course illusory, and even the illusion showed only in high places. Men and women still lived lives for the most part shaped between the 3rd century B.C. and the Reformation; history was still transmitted, only its rate had changed; tradition was still manifest and available, only some of the modes of its expression needed renewal to meet the actual situation. What had crumbled was not the will and the imagination, but the belief in the will and in the daringness or passion of the imagination.

The optimism of materialism dumped great rampages of energy noisily into the sink of inertia; only the pessimist had the will and the passion to struggle for images—for symbols—in which to create the human significance—the significance to humans—out of the energies which moved him and which, as he aspired to affirm himself, he must move.[8]

I should point out at this point that Blackmur is following Adams's practice of casting historical movements in personal, psychological terms, thereby creating a dramatic moving narrative which is also in the manner of the French historian Michelet. In following this procedure, Blackmur carefully balances inner reactions with outer forces in an attempt to show the human significance of history. This procedure also attempts to recenter man in the flow of impersonal history. It was Adams's task, Blackmur believed, to restore belief in the human will and imagination by finding a new symbolic language for the new cultural energies.

Unfortunately, the kind of mind Adams had predisposed him to experience culture in a certain way inimical to his task. "Failure," Blackmur writes,

is the appropriate end to the type of mind of which Adams is a preeminent example: the type which attempts through imagination to find the meaning or source of unity aside from the experience which it unites. . . . Failure, far from incidental, is integral to that attempt, and becomes apparent just so soon as reason falters and becomes abstract, or faith fails and pretends to be absolute. . . . What differentiates Adams' mind from other minds engaged in the same effort is his own intense and progressive recognition of his failure; and that recognition springs from the same overload of scruples that made him eccentric to the society that produced him.[9]

Instead of seeking unity in his *experience* of culture, Adams sought unity outside of his experience in a symbol. In other words Adams looked solely outside himself to the external forces impinging upon him for the unity that had also to emerge from within. Besides looking in the wrong place for his unity, Adams's rational search for a symbol negated the nature and purpose of a symbol. Symbols, Blackmur says, cannot be looked for rationally but must come to the surface of the emotional furnace by themselves.

True symbols, in the sense that the term is used here, are the means by which we express our understanding, or our helplessness in understanding, of what we cannot articulate verbally or by any other intellectual means. Symbols actually accrete and store the power with which we credit them, and become the more inexhaustible of that power the more they are used, providing the user still feels within himself what that power is. But true symbols cannot do the work of the intellect, and whenever the intellect either is actually able to do the work of the symbol, or deludes itself that it can do so, the power of the symbol disappears. Thus the validity and necessity of symbols depend on the human situation in which the mind realizes that it is dealing with energies beyond its descriptive knowledge or that it is helpless under the pressure of energies of which it has no direct knowledge at all. This was the human situation of Henry Adams. Neither the descriptive laws of energy made by his own age nor the symbols which happened to survive from the last age seemed to him adequate to cope with the energies he actually felt at work. Nor did the private symbols he had discovered in his own life satisfy his needs once he put them in full context.[10]

Blackmur's view, then, is that Adams went about his search in the wrong way; that is, rationally, consciously looking for a symbol which would unite inner and outer forces when the symbol he sought could appear only organically, rising to the surface of his emotional furnace. Further, Blackmur claims, Adams knew that his methodology would make him fail; yet, acknowledging that the interpretative task needed at least to be attempted, Adams went ahead. The record of his attempt, Blackmur says, is in the successive artistic forms in which he tried to express his experience of the new cultural forces. The record includes two novels, *Democracy* and *Esther,* and two companion books of essays, *Mont-Saint-Michel and Chartres* and *The Education of Henry Adams.*

Adams's two novels by themselves, Blackmur says, would hardly be worth reading "except to satisfy an omnivorous taste in the detritus of the third quarter of nineteenth century American fiction."[11] They are valuable only as records. Adams turned to novel-writing after modest success with the essay form. He had published *The Life of Albert Gallatin* in 1879 and a biography of John Randolph in 1882. The novels were published just before and just after, *Democracy* in 1880 and *Esther* in 1884. Blackmur believes that the novels must be viewed as experiments in aesthetic form.

If a man cannot act upon his dilemma, or escape it in blind action, he will sometimes attempt to make symbols or fables of what would otherwise drive him to action; and it is as such symbols, such fables, that Adams' two novels best clarify themselves. It is, I think, to a considerable extent how he meant them, and it is certainly how we may best use them for ourselves. They show what were to become twenty years later his major themes slowly, rather lamely, and with many concessions of a superfluous sort to the "exigencies" of the popular novel, taking their first imaginative form, the one as judgment and the other as the beginning of prophecy.[12]

The principal character in *Democracy* is Madeleine Lee, "a widow of thirty with twenty-odd thousand a year, attractive, intelligent, and well-connected, but with a degree of naivete, who comes to Washington with her younger sister, Sybil, because she is bored with New York and Boston and social Europe." Madeleine has an interest in learning how the country is really run. She meets various members of Washington society and falls in love with Senator Ratcliffe of Illinois, who is the real power in Washington. During the course of the novel, Adams dutifully chronicles the corruption in American government and the sterility of political life. Senator Ratcliffe, of course, has a hand in many and various political and financial machinations. At first Madeleine Lee thinks that Ratcliffe is a man of scruples who must deal with scoundrels. Her recognition of his true moral view and values is the dramatic climax of the novel and Blackmur's main point of interest. At the last meeting between Madeleine and Ratcliffe, Madeleine refuses his offer of marriage with the explanation that they lead different lives. The crucial difference is in their moral point of view. Ratcliffe can see nothing wrong in his accepting a bribe for the good of the party. Madeleine, on the other hand, has no clear moral point of view, only an aversion to Ratcliffe's. This fact, says Blackmur, marks the essential failing in the novel. Madeleine, as a persona for Adams, had no moral point of view because Adams himself had none.

Adams, hovering between his two worlds, had as yet no clear answer, no answer that he could stick to, nor have the liberals today. Pure intelligence still coquettes with the corruption which it fears, is still unwilling to cleanse necessity by performing it, but asks corruption rather to reform itself first, and then flies to its great pyramid and its pole star when corruption refuses the wooden nutmeg of reform [a reference to Senator French in the novel, who is the representative of Connecticut, the Nutmeg State].[13]

The essential literary problem is that Adams adopted a form ill-suited to his desire to express the new cultural energies. He thought that in a novel of politics he could capture and symbolize the essence of the basically secular forces he perceived and that political Washington might be the new emotional symbol he was seeking. Blackmur's complaint that the novel fails is grounded in his judgment that the form cannot contain what Adams wanted to put into it. Or, put into the terms of Blackmur's poetic theory, Adams's reason cannot or was unable at the time to find a form adequate to the imaginative expression of the emotion he felt. This is the critical judgment implicit in Blackmur's statement that the lesson to be learned from *Democracy* insofar as it is an example of Adams's experimentation in aesthetic form is that "it shows the intelligence which is willing to tamper with the actual without being willing to seize it, as properly humiliated and sent flying. If the failure of Madeleine lay deeper than that," Blackmur continues, "it was perhaps that she never understood the principle that the intelligence must always act as if it were adequate to the problems it has aroused. That is, it must see the evils it attacks as the vivid forms of its own abused and debased self. Otherwise it must give up."[14]

In *Esther* Adams used the novel form again but this time investigated the possibilities of a religious context. If the Virgin as a symbol derived its power from religion, then perhaps a similar symbol might be found in modern religion. Esther Dudley, the heroine, "is a young woman with a high taste in art and a high achievement in humanity, serious, with a conscience, an intelligence, and an infinitely malleable sensibility; she needs only a mastering faith to generate conviction and strength."[15] Once again, the lead character may be taken as a persona for Adams. The drama in this novel, as in *Democracy*, is provided by the clash of opposing ideas, in this instance embodied in the Episcopal minister Stephan Hazard and the geologist George Strong. Science and religion fight for Esther's soul. In Adams's mind, however, science and religion at bottom call for the same kind of trust or faith in something mysterious and incomprehensible in the universe. Thus, Blackmur says, the opposing forces vying for Esther's soul are but two different manifestations of the same thing. Like Madeleine, Esther fails to find something to affirm. Hazard, who argues for the Church, finally appeals to "the natural instincts" of Esther's sex. To this plea she answers: "Why must the church always appeal to my weakness and never to my strength: I ask for spiritual life and you send me back to my flesh and blood as though I were a tigress you were sending back to her cubs." The Church's appeal to instinct is its failing. Adams discovered, Blackmur says, that the intelligent man

found himself in the desperate position of having to give up, at the critical moment, and no matter which faith he chose, intelligence itself. That was perhaps because, in that energetic age, he mistook faith for a superior form of energy, like coal power or water power or atomic power, rather than for a primitive—or fundamental—form of insight. The poor fellow wanted to transcend himself by calling upon a higher energy, when he ought rather to have tried to discover the faith of what he actually was.[16]

If Adams could have perceived faith as a fundamental form of insight and focused it on his experience of culture, he might have found the unity he was seeking. But, and this was the point, religion offered (at least in Adams's time) unity for a price and that price was rationality—the working intelligence.

Taken together, Blackmur writes, the novels were "rather fables of the inconclusive; complementary to each other, they represented the gropings of a maturing mind after its final theme. Taken together they mark the turning point of a mind which had constructed itself primarily for a life of political action into a new life which should be predominately imaginative and prophetic."[17] The main difference between the two novels was that "where *Democracy* dealt with man in his relation to society in terms of existing institutions which, whether they controlled or failed to control political power, at least represented it, *Esther* reached out to seize, to bring to rebirth, the spiritual power which the existing church, as Adams saw it in 1883, represented only a kind of betrayal in terms of Pilate's position."[18] The most interesting similarity between the two novels is that the leading characters are women. Blackmur points out that Adams's choice of women to be the principals in his novels reflected a major bias of his imagination. "Women, for Adams, had instinct and emotion and could move from the promptings of the one to the actualities of the other without becoming lost or distraught in the midway bog of logic and fact."[19] In this respect, Adams thought that women were some-how the key to the unity of forces he was seeking. But if the search for unity eluded him, he was sure that the novelistic form would not suit his purposes.

In one last great imaginative effort, Adams wrote two books which he meant to be read as united in concept and as a planned work of the imagination. In Chapter 29 of *The Education*, written in the third person, Adams explained his unifying concept.

Any schoolboy could see that man as a force must be measured by motion, from a fixed point. Psychology helped here by suggesting a unit—the point of history when man held the highest idea of himself as a unit in a unified universe. Eight or ten years of study had led Adams to think he might use the century 1150-1250, expressed in Amiens Cathedral and the Works of Thomas Aquinas, as the unit from which he might measure motion down to his own time, without assuming anything as true or untrue, except relation. The movement might be studied at once in philosophy and mechanics. Setting himself to the task, he began a volume which he mentally knew as "Mont-Saint-Michel and Chartres: a Study of Thirteenth Century Unity." From that point he proposed to fix a position for himself, which he could label: "The Education of Henry Adams: A Study of Twentieth Century Multiplicity." With the help of these two points of relation, he hoped to project his lines forward and backward indefinitely, subject to correction from anyone who should know better.

Adams's general purpose in these two books, Blackmur says, was "to make types and symbols in permanent form of Adams' effort to respond and assent to his own time."[20] Adams was convinced, Blackmur continues, that for a century, 1150-1250,

the emotional symbolism of Christian culture penetrated and enriched the recesses of the whole being, in terms of actual values felt, whereas the meaning of scientific and economic law did not penetrate but flattened out the beings who suffered from their operation, and did so precisely because the powers they dealt with had not been translated or expressed in adequate symbolic form. It was therefore natural that, feeling within him both the old and the new energies, and rediscovering for himself the vitality of the old symbols, he should attempt to discover symbols which could express his vital relationship with the new energies, and that, further, he should attempt to feel both sets of symbols together and in their relations.[21]

To Adams, the symbol of the Virgin represented the unity of mind and spirit in the thirteenth century. The unity, Blackmur says, was "the harmony of true liberalism" or the elasticity in thirteenth-century Christian culture that enabled it to embrace different and contradictory modes of human expression. Adams wrote:

A church which embraced with equal sympathy, and within a hundred years, the Virgin, Saint Bernard, William of Champeaux and the School of Saint Victor, Peter the Venerable, Saint Francis of Assisi, Saint Dominic, Saint Thomas of Aquinas, and Saint Bonaventure was more liberal than any modern state can afford to be. Radical contradictions the State may perhaps tolerate, though hardly, but never embrace or profess. Such elasticity long ago vanished from human thought.

The church embraced scholastic logic and the irrational rapture of Francis; it created an inner harmony between reason and imagination, between intuition and the reasonable search for truth; and above it all was the unifying symbol of the Virgin. "The Queen Mother," Adams wrote in Chapter 6 of *Chartres,*

was as majestic as you like: she was absolute; she could be stern; she was not above being angry; but she was still a woman, who loved grace, beauty, ornament, . . . who considered the arrangements of her palace with attention, and liked both light and colour; who kept a keen eye on her Court, and extracted prompt and willing obedience from king and archbishops as well as from beggars and drunken priests. She protected her friends and punished her enemies. She required space, beyond what was known in Courts of kings, because she was liable at all times to have ten thousand people begging her favors—mostly inconsistent with law—and deaf to refusal. She was extremely sensitive to neglect, to disagreeable impressions, to want of intelligence in her surroundings. She was the greatest artist, as she was the greatest philosopher and musician and theologist, that ever lived on earth, except her Son, Who, at Chartres, is still an enfant under her guardianship. Her taste was infallible; her silence eternally final. This church was built for her in this spirit of simple-minded, practical, utilitarian faith,—in this singleness of thought, exactly as a little girl sets up a doll house for her favorite blonde doll. Unless you can go back to your dolls, you are out of place here. If you can go back to them, and get rid of one small hour of the weight of custom, you shall see Chartres in glory.

In the symbol of the Virgin, Adams recognized that unity is possible through emotion even when denied by reason; that intuition may triumph over logic and that art may penetrate deeper into the mysteries of experience than science.

Turning to his own age, Adams sought a similar symbol for twentieth-century multiplicity. He found, however, that symbols in this century are not the irrational creations of the emotions; instead, they are rational creations insufficient in emotional power to express or be symbols for the new cultural energies. Adams considered the symbol of the dynamo in *The Education* and wrote: "Before the end, one began to pray to it; inherited instinct taught the natural expression of man before silent and infinite force." But the dynamo as symbol was unsatisfactory, and in his later years Adams adopted the law of entropy in a final attempt to find unity. "It was," Blackmur writes, "the theory of a desperate, weary mind, still scrupulous in desperation and passionately eager in weariness, in its last effort to feel—this time in nature itself—the mystery in energy that keeps things going."[22] But Adams's whole effort to find a symbol and a form that would be emotionally satisfying—that would create and *stand for* a psychological harmony within man—was bound to fail in a rational age. As Blackmur expressed it:

The chasm between the self which creates and the symbol created has always been great, and was bound to be especially so in an age which tried for legal description and literal authority and which created its symbols either as convenient slogans, or inadvertently, or under the illusion that they were descriptions: *Laissez faire*, survival of the fittest, or the laws of thermodynamics, none of which was the source of the values each engaged, but each of which superseded and confounded the energy of the values which should have illuminated them. As symbols, such phrases failed because each claimed in little to describe accurately, literally, authoritatively some vast field of human or natural energy; each asserted itself equal to its field; none held in reserve the power of the occult, the mysterious, the unknowable; none, in short, was itself, as well as what it stood for.[23]

III   *Adams's Importance to Blackmur*

Adams's perception of his culture and his reaction to that perception made him Blackmur's archetypal artist-critic. Since Blackmur believed that both artist and critic had to make an aesthetic response to their society, the conditions and terms of that response became all important. To Blackmur's generation, Henry Adams was the only one who had left such a rational, conscious record of his aesthetic response to his society. Adams tried to make sense out of what was happening to him, and the social conditions he perceived were the same as those perceived by Blackmur. Basically, they both envisioned society as an amalgam of competing forces without meaning and both assumed that to establish meaning one needed a framework, a form, a point of view. Underlying this assumption was another more fundamental assumption, that human beings seek order, harmony, and meaning in their lives. Both had an eighteenth-century faith in reason, yet both had seen enough of rationalism in science to be sceptical of the ultimate efficacy of reason.

Both believed that any framework of meaning would be temporary and eventually cast aside. Blackmur seems to have been very impressed with Adams's intellectual fastidiousness on this point and it follows from his essays on the critic's job that had Adams been otherwise, Blackmur would have thought him guilty of doctrinaire thinking. Yet in the matter of choosing an adequate framework Adams faced a problem common to all modern artists, and a problem which constantly confronted Blackmur as critic. The problem was that the institutions that had hitherto given meaningful frameworks to experience were in decline and no longer viable as sources for artistic inspiration. Institutions like the church and the state had once provided a political, economic, and, most importantly, a metaphysical framework which the artist *lived in* and could *draw upon* for the subject matter of his art. In modern times these frameworks were still around but were not spiritually satisfactory. The task of the critic, Blackmur believed, was to discover which modern institutions or ideas could supply frameworks of meaning. This was the problem Adams also faced, and Blackmur was intensely interested to see how he had handled it.

From his own thinking Blackmur knew several things about handling this problem. He knew that the framework of meaning or what he came to call a "rival creation" could not be created solely from within the emotional-intellectual cumulus of the artist-critic's own mind. It would be too idiosyncratic, too personal, and Blackmur never liked "private" meaning whether in poetry or in abstractions. So, the source of a rival creation—a framework of meaning—also had to come from outside the mind of the critic. It had to be something recognizably derived from the culture and internalized just enough to be emotionally satisfying. On this point, Blackmur was again very impressed with Adams's description of the Virgin of Chartres. But the Virgin could only be a paradigm for the twentieth century. The problem for our own time remained—from where could meaning be derived? Blackmur also know that rival creations are not derived rationally, although they may subsequently satisfy man's need for a rational explanation of his experience and may themselves be rationally described. In the beginning, when a framework of meaning is created, it is born of the rational-imagination—that paradoxical, contradictory *thing* which Blackmur claimed was a fusion of reason and imagination in sensibility. This sensibility is associated with the mystical and the religious and is hardly allowed in rational discourse, yet Blackmur believed as Adams did that it was only this kind of sensibility that could discover unity.

But how does one get to this unity? How long must the quest be? In religion a ceremony surrounds and encases the perception of the sacred; in art, a form surrounds and encases the critic's perception of the content. If the content is the search for unity the perception of which will provide a framework of meaning, then the form which leads to that perception is important. For the ceremony to work, the forms must be followed. Blackmur was interested in Adams's two novels because they were forms Adams had followed to arrive at a perception of unity. No perception of unity came, so he discarded the forms. And still Adams continued on and Blackmur watched, following the evidence of the written word. Adams found no unity and no form that he was satisfied would lead him to unity.

With no permanent insight coming from Adams, Blackmur could only leave him and follow his own path, seeking a solution, an insight, a perception into unity through investigations of literary form. The perception of unity—of a framework of meaning that would satisfy the emotional and rational needs of men—was necessary to his criticism because only then could he have and give the conviction to artists and to society that he believed was necessary for great art. In personal terms, to gain the perception he sought, Blackmur had to begin reacting to his own experience with more imagination and less reason so as to balance them out. His essays began to be prose poems and his critical judgments began to sound like emotional, poetic utterances encased in the restraining framework of a critical essay on a particular work. Throughout all of his later work, his essays are related to his search for a unity; and the more obscure they appear to a rational mind, the closer Blackmur got to his goal. In his later years, Blackmur quoted two phrases that denoted for him what he was doing: "I am an ignorant man, almost a poet," and "Art bitten by poetry longs to be freed from reason." The phrases were symbolic of a life's work to achieve a condition in himself that was as mysterious, irrational, and yet as harmonious as that achieved in the poetry of Wallace Stevens. And Henry Adams was Blackmur's guide to this end.

CHAPTER 5

Blackmur's "Loose and Baggy Monsters"

ARMED with an intellectual and emotional point of view derived from and developed during his study of Henry Adams, Blackmur turned his attention in the 1940s and 1950s to the European novel. Like Henry James, Blackmur found the European novel more aesthetically satisfying than the contemporary American and English novel because it was more intimately involved with society. To Blackmur, the American and English novel was too "private," too idiosyncratic in imagery and symbol to fulfill a purpose he envisioned for it. Blackmur wanted his novels to provide "either a new psychology or a theoretic form of life."[1] In certain European novels, Blackmur found examples of the kind of writing, intimately involved with society, that provided a new psychology for its time and a new way of perceiving life. Henry James, in his preface to *The Tragic Muse*, called such novels "large loose baggy monsters." To James and to Blackmur, novels were so designated when, in addition to their structural excellence, they embodied the culture of which they were a part.

In his essays on the European novel, Blackmur developed his own critical idiom to denote the critical framework he had developed in his study of Adams. He did not believe that his particular idiom was obscure and arcane, but he did believe that his readers would have to do their own critic's job of work in reading these essays on the novel. This belief stemmed from his conception of the critical essay as a work of art. The essays under review here, then, present a special idiom and framework of meaning that must be defined before an understanding of them is possible.

Blackmur believed in a life-force that was the essence of all

things and of which all eein; were a manifestation. Blackmur's
life-force is much like Bergson's *élan vital*, Hegel's *Zeitgeist*,
Adams's unity, or the Buddhist concept of Brahman. Blackmur
adopted the term *Numen* for this life-force.

The *Numen* or *numinosus* is that power within us, greater than and
other than ourselves, that moves us, sometimes carrying us away, in the
end moving us forward unless we drop out, always overwhelming us. So
far as it may be felt in literature it resembles the force of the sublime
described by Longinus—the blow that transports us. It is a force
sometimes cultivated as magic, as superstition, as mystery: it is related
to rhythm which gives meaning to action. Religion has always cultivated
this force with the piety of excruciated sense, and religion has always
taken it as the spring of absolute, or rational, action—not the action but
its spring, as the Incarnation or the Crucifixion. Thus the *Numen* enters,
though it is not itself, behavior. It is the reality that presses into
behavior but never reaches whole incarnation there.[2]

The life-force, the Numen, is the vital, flowing energy that
permeates all things. It is in humans and in inanimate objects like
churches and paintings; and also in ideas and institutions like
Christianithand the Church. The Numen is a refinement of
Blackmur's earlier concept of gesture. His primary interest in
Numen is in its individual human and in its social manifestations.
In these guises Blackmur calls it by several different names in
particular critical essays, but he means the same thing and it is
analogous to Adams's concept of forces. Numen is manifested in
humans through forms called "manners." Manners may be
understood on the individual or on the collective level as forms
of human behavior. "Behavior" is a Blackmurian term for what
humans as individuals and as masses of individuals do—how they
act—and a term also for how they react. In society and in
individual action, manners are the forms for human behavior and
are themselves a manifestation of Numen.

Blackmur believed that individuals not only were permeated
with Numen but also responded to it and that these responses
were in set patterns of behavior; or, in other words, modes or
manners of behavior. Analogous to language in his poetic theory,
manners of behavior may also be or become old, trite,
hackneyed, and therefore in need of an infusion of vitality, which
is to say, an infusion of Numen. As the fundamental essence,
Numen has vinali6indand revitalizing powers which the manners

of human behavior may sometimes block. When this happens, a new manner of behavior must be tried or discovered by the individual or by the whole society that reestablishes the flow of Numen, or as Blackmur sometimes calls it, actuality. Numen, actuality, reality—in Blackmur's mind these terms refer to the same idea—has another important attribute in addition to its ubiquity. It is, he says, equivocal. It has no meaning and no ethics. Metaphysical and ethical systems are intellectual overlays which men seem to need in order to live. One other important characteristic of Numen is that it is in motion. Blackmur conceptualized this motion as a continual emotional and social turbulence that he called momentum. To summarize, Numen is that raw, elemental force which permeates all things but which by itself has no meaning and no ethics. Constantly in motion, Numen is manifested in human beings through their behavior, which is in the form of manners. To give an example of the difference between behavior and manner I could say that killing someone is the behavior while *how* it is done, quickly with a gun or slowly over many years through various means, is the manner.

Opposed to Numen and completing Blackmur's critical terminology is the concept he called *Moha*. Moha is a Sanskrit word that he defined as

a term for the basic, irremediable, irreplaceable, characteristic, and contemptuous stupidity of man confronted with choice or purpose . . . [it] also refers to the stubborn tenacity of will—of blind necessary action—by which man puts up with what is intolerable in his life. . . . But perhaps the central meaning of the term is reflected in its history. *Moha* is from a language which grew in a land where cattle are both sacred and obstacles to rational action; much as our pastoral terms came from a land of sheep and goats. *Moha* means cow: the cow that fattens off the land and has the right of way in any traffic. Thus by analogy the word contains all we mean by "sheepish" in look or in gesture, but it means it in action and fundamental nature. It is Pasiphäe become a cow, the cow that is in all of us, as Dante observes in his Purgatory. It is what our behavior, unenlightened and unimpeded, would leave us at. It is what we are like when we deprive ourselves of the three things reason requires of beauty: *consonantia, integritas, claritas:* harmony, wholeness, radiance.[3]

Moha is a term, then, for instinctual human nature and instinctual human behavior without the modifying effects of reason.

In Blackmur's critical framework, life and literature fall between the two extremes represented by Numen and Moha. With this framework Blackmur wants to do more than just judge novels, he wants to use it to explain the genesis of society and the genesis of literature and its relationship to society. Society is created, he says, out of humanity's response "to the turbulence of actual life."[4] "Indeed," he continues,

in that response is the source of social structures and of morals themselves; for that response is the rational insistence of the individual on his right to survive no matter what the obstacles. Literature is our account of such survivals and failures to survive. Literature is our theoretic struggle with behavior; but we feed on what we fight and move in the form of our struggle. For behavior gets into literature as the outward and sensible form of our momentum, the forces which carry us on, some our own, and some alien to us: some the breathing of our dearest selves, some the air that suffocates us. . . . Thus we see in literature the constant effort to create new forms of order, new theoretic forms for the conflict, or the fusion, of the reality which is revelation or epiphany, never wholly known, and that other reality which compels behavior and is never completely manifest. This is our effort to find theoretic forms for the struggle in us between the alleluia and the hallelujah, between the *Numen* and the Moha.

In life and therefore in literature there are two great human questions: "What can one do to live a spiritually fulfilling life?" and "How does one act?" The first is a metaphysical question, the second is an ethical one. Blackmur believed that humans reached their fullest potential when they were attuned to and conscious of Numen. He never gave an explicit explanation of what a human at his fullest potential was like but it was something like being in a mystic harmony with Numen. One achieved this transcendence through the two great faculties of the mind—reason and imagination in combination or fused together as the rational imagination. The answer to the ethical question "How does one act?" is perhaps more important in Blackmur's critical framework because it involves the essence of the social fabric which is the subject matter of the novel. He believed that the institutions of Western civilization, its laws, written and unwritten, its religion, and its arts were forms of human behavior, that is, morals in action. To Blackmur, one's morals, how one decided to act, had a direct bearing on society and further, the aggregate of moral actions taken by individuals became codified in society by law, art, or religion.

The social institutions of society are important in Blackmur's critical framework. In addition to the forms known as law, art, and religion, social forms may also be theoretical constructs like Idealism, Materialism, Christianity, Diabolism, and so forth. The function of all these forms once they become codified and when taken together may be said to represent a society, aculture, eroviding a metaphysical and ethical framework in which man as an individual can act or react. In Blackmur's view, modern Western culture is at a transition point between the old Greco-Christian heritage and some new heritage Adams sought in the representative symbol of the dynamo. Blackmur believed that the European novelists would discover and announce this new heritage first because they seemed to him to be expressly looking for it in the conditions of their social experience. He looked to the conceptual frameworks in the novels of Thomas Mann, Gustave Flaubert, James Joyce, Leo Tolstoy, and Feodor Dostoevski to discover the new and developing Western heritage because he believed that their masterpieces "gradually reveal themselves by the uses to which we are forced to put them, as philosophies, religions, politics—and as the therapies and prophecies of these."[5] And, Blackmur continues,

This seems to have happened only partly in the sense that the arts have tried to take over the *functions* of these modes of mind; it has happened much more in the sense that the *experience* of these modes of the mind has become the most pressing part of the subject matter of the arts. It is not the artist's fault if his audience insists on confusing function and experience by the special arrogance of ignorance and the special vanity of uncommittedness in relation to existing society. The point is, our masterpieces are therapy and prophecy, though they cure nothing present and envisage nothing future. They see and state. And of course, with the formal advantages that go with the arts, they state better than they see.

On an individual level, Blackmur believed that more and more people, spiritually stagnated by the old forms of culture would seek to recapture the vitalizing flow and infusion of Numen in behavioral forms of their own making. Since it was and is possible that these new forms could become the basis for new cultural forms, he paid particular attention to those novels in which a character was faced with or forced into a different life-style. In the particular novels he chose to review, the new behavioral forms of characters represent their creator's conceptual frameworks of meaning; or, in other words, their way of ordering their experience of Numen. In effect, then, Blackmur claimed that these novelists in experiencing Numen directly rather than through the old forms of culture, were having experiences exactly like those that are termed religious and/or aesthetic experiences. And since society, culture, and literature are created from the response "to the turbulence of actual life," he felt that it was absolutely crucial that the audience of these novelists understand what was going on in the novels. He perceived, however, that the audience was alienated from art and artists and had confused in their own lives the actual experience of the Numen with their experience of it in the novel; and, as a consequence, had used novels, and the arts in general, as symbols of the cultural sickness and also as remedies for it. The arts are for aesthetic purposes only, Blackmur believed, not for functional purposes. But the result of the confusion on the audience's part is a "gap" that is the critic's function to bridge. In a passage which illustrates his later style, delineates the purpose of art in our time, defines the spiritual consequences of the decline of the old forms of Numen, and which by extrapolation intimates the role of the critic, Blackmur wrote:

Like the gap between heart beats, between the words of a message, or between the votes cast and the candidate elected, it is the distance between the idea and reality which must always be crossed if work is to be done; public and private life both depend on crossing it. Yet what lies between is what actually goes on. The life of action cannot afford direct familiarity with it, but cannot lose relevance to it except at great peril. With the arts it is the other way round. The arts take no action and do not seek directly to change the world; their domain is precisely the actual experience of what goes on between the idea and the reality; but they must nevertheless, if they are to escape the condition of total flux or total chaos, hold some implicit allegiance to the idea as intent and to the reality as aspiration. When the imaginations devoted to the life of action—religion, ethics, philosophy, politics—break down or become inadequate or distrust themselves, there is a double consequence in the arts. They become either abstract or too much in the flux, and they find themselves taking on as part of actual experience—like an injured heart, a halting breath, an hysterical speech—the breakdown, inadequacy, and distrust. In T. S. Eliot's phrase, you get an incredible public world and an intolerable private world. The arts can deal with the quality, the actuality, of such a world only with difficulty and intermittently, and so to speak by falling back upon their own momentum. Because there is too much for the artist to do and too little for the audience to bring, there is a failure of relation between the artist and his art and between the art and its audience; and the gaps widen.[6]

I   Anna Karenina

Blackmur's practical application of his critical framework produced some rather unique insights. *Anna Karenina,* Tolstoy's novel about a society woman who leaves her husband for a lover and who finally kills herself, has been viewed by some critics as a well-written but over-blown melodramatic social tragedy. In Blackmur's hands, however, the novel takes on its real significance and power as a work of art in a social context.

Blackmur's theme in this essay, subtitled "The Dialectic of Incarnation," is based upon his belief that Numen is often blocked by old forms of behavior and that to unblock Numen and consequently revitalize one's behavior, an individual has to seek new forms of behavior—that is, he must seek new manners. Blackmur focuses, then, on how Anna tries to change her behavior—change her life—in an attempt to rediscover the forces of life which the old forms of her behavior had kept from her.

"Each individual life," Blackmur begins, "and also that life in fellowship which we call society are so to speak partial incarnations of that force [Numen]; but neither is ever complete; thus the great human struggle, for the individual or for society, is so to react and so to respond to 'the terrible ambiguity of an immediate experience' as to approach the conditions of rebirth, the change of heart, or even the fresh start. Tragedy comes about from the failure to apprehend the character or the direction of that force, either by an exaggeration of the self alone or of the self in society." Anna's motivation to leave her husband, Karenin, stems not from her love for Vronsky, Blackmur says, but from her need to revitalize her life, to reopen the channels of Numen. Her love for Vronsky, then, is a means to an end, an

opportunity to change her manner of behavior in the hopes of
living a more satisfying life.

Manners are important to Blackmur because they "are the
medium in which the struggle between the institution of society
and the needs of individuals is conducted. . . . When in
imagination or dogma the institutions are seen to triumph the
manners become hollow, cold, and cruel. When the needs of the
individual triumph the manners tend to disappear, so that life
together becomes impossible." Manners serve two basic human
purposes; they are the forms, the vessels, in which we receive
Numen, and they are the social lubricant of society. Put another
way, they are that by which we know ourselves and that by
which we relate to others. But there is a constant friction
between the two purposes, Blackmur says, and in this novel "it is
through the manners that the needs and possibilities of each
person are seen in shifting conflict with the available or relevant
institutions, including the twilight institutions—the illicit, amorphous institutions—which stand at the edges of the institutions of
broad day."

Having fallen in love with Count Vronsky, Anna's behavior
changes and her manner, her habitual forms of action which
include the way she acts toward her husband, also changes.
Karenin feels this change in his wife's manner and reacts by
asking her to consider the consequences of her affair. In the
confrontation that takes place in their bedroom after Anna has
returned late one night from seeing Vronsky, Tolstoy dramatically portrays the friction between the stultifying manners
of society embodied in Karenin that block the flow of Numen and
the emerging new manners embodied in Anna that release
Numen. "He who had always worked with reflections of life, and
had shrunk away from life itself as something irrational and
incomprehensible, now found himself 'standing face to face with
life.' In attempting to deceive him she makes the mistake of
being natural, candid, light hearted, qualities which in the
circumstance are effects of the unseen force."

Her affair with Vronsky, her new manners of behavior,
revitalize Anna's life; unfortunately, Blackmur says, her new
behavior hinders rather than helps her relationship with society.
The very motivation that led her to escape an unsatisfying,
unfulfilling life has now led her into different circumstances
equally as unsatisfying for different reasons. There is a symbiotic
relationship, Blackmur believes, between an individual and his

society. In Anna's new circumstances, living with Vronsky, separated from her husband but not divorced, the spiritually nourishing aspects of society are denied her. "Without the aid, rather the enmity, of decorum, manners, institutions, they cannot cope with the now-visible force that binds *and* splits them. . . . Anna tries, and puts off trying, to join together the shame, rapture, and horror of 'stepping into a new life.'" It is perhaps paradoxical that with a new manner and therefore a closer grasp of reality—a rebirth, a new infusion of Numen—Anna cannot stand alone. She needs some society, some institutional forms of behavior, which she can relate to. She is ostracized and Vronsky assumes the former role played by her husband, Karenin—he embodies the accepted forms of social behavior and metaphorically breaks Anna's back as he literally breaks that of his horse Frou-Frou in the steeplechase.

For Blackmur, the character Anna Karenina is emblematic of modern man's search for new forms of behavior which will put him in a new relationship with Numen, which in turn will revitalize himself and society. In Anna's case, she found a new form and was reincarnated, though not completely, Blackmur says, into a new self that was "proper to her own nature." With her new self, Anna faced the problem of how to live with a morality in which the highest good was spiritual self-sufficiency. But Anna was unable to be self-sufficient because in negating the old forms of behavior she had but one new form in which to hold all of the inflowing of Numen that opened up to her. That one form was her love for Vronsky, but it was not large enough to suffice. She was then left with a choice either to return to the old forms of behavior, where her spirit would be deadened but where she would have the assent of society, or to let Numen take hold of her completely. In committing suicide she chose the latter. "Her tragedy," Blackmur writes, "is that she has destroyed too much of the medium, too many of the possibilities, of actual life, to leave life tolerable, and she has done this partly by dissociating manners from the actual world and partly by losing her sense of the sweep of things. Thus her last turning point, her last effort at incarnation, was death."

II Madame Bovary

Like Anna, Emma Bovary is seeking a new vitality through new manners of behavior. But where Anna's motivation derived from her love for Vronsky, Emma's derives, Blackmur says, from Bovarysme. Blackmur acknowledges the dictionary definition of Bovarysme: domination by a romantic conception of the self; but adds that "this is an English or American sentimental version of what the word ought to define. Bovarysme is an habitual, an infatuated practice of regarding, not the self, but the world as other than it is." Emma regards the world in images of romantic passion and this is the motivating force behind her seeking new manners of behavior. There is something else about Emma that makes her special and unique as a personality. She has an openness, a predilection to try new forms of behavior that Blackmur calls her "beauty out of place."

She has all the energy of beauty out of place with which to transform the illicit, the prodigal, the nostalgic from the low price, narrow motives, and contemptible manners in which she finds them: the maximum against which the adolescent can compete. Emma's energy is of the highest price: the high price of beauty out of place raised still higher by hysteria. Beauty out of place will always be marred; its efforts at self-assertion and self-protection must always be excessive, since it must create its object as well as its response to it, and when the object fails comes hysteria: the disease or disorder which is the convulsive effort of the womb that cannot create. . . . Her beauty is the name we give to what in Emma is deeply corrupted but what even in death is itself uncorrupting: it is the vital, rising, buoyant quality of her response to life.

Emma's response to life, to the Numen, takes the forms of her successive relationships beginning with her husband, Charles, through Rodolphe, her first lover, and ending with Leon, her second lover. Throughout these various relationships there is an undercurrent in Emma's personality that drives her on—the current of herself as a force channeled into the illusion of romantic passion. She enters into her marriage with Charles, Blackmur says, "as a beginning, as something additional, as a realization of the unknown." Very soon the romantic illusion of marriage gives way to the ennui of the quotidian. But it is precisely in their illusions about marriage that the reader sees the essential difference between them.

Charles' vision of the world and of Emma and his conduct toward both—his loyalty, trust, love, tenderness, industry—are all locked up in an attempt which is also a need for an infatuated version of what ought to be. His security in that vision depends on what is "lawful" turning out to be right and not only right but effective. Emma's security depends not on rebellion against the lawful, nor on denial of law, but on her capacity for taking advantage of the lawful at another level than Charles—precisely the level of the illicit—the wrongdoing which the law prescribes by definition. She creates herself in the very imperfections laid out by law and found in literature and art as images of passion and the infatuation of passion. Charles is nothing without the law, Emma is nothing except outside the law.

Charles finds the fulfillment of his being in the manners of behavior that have come to be traditional in the relationship between two married people. Emma, however, because of her "beauty out of place," can only find fulfillment through the unlawful, the untraditional, in marriage. Numen, manifested for her in the illusion of romantic passion, is what she seeks; and her actions, her behavior, must become unlawful in adultery. Like Anna's Vronsky, Emma's Rodolphe is the means to an end. In her relationship with him she hopes to find the ideal of romantic passion. As it had been with Charles, her being is fulfilled for a time until the ideal of passion, the force of her response to Numen takes over and Rodolphe is to her a form to be filled. "Her love for Rodolphe," Blackmur writes, "becomes at this time a convulsive creation of her hysteria, and at the same moment destroys in Rodolphe all that had been actual in his feeling for her. He is now the creation of her passion; she is now the creature of his lust. She involves herself to the limit; he extricates himself. She steals to buy him gifts and begins her social destruction. He coolly promotes the immediate possibilities."

Rodolphe soon leaves, and the force of Numen in the guise of romantic passion begins to permeate Emma's being. "Emma remains accessible to experience, to invasion, destruction, hysteria, to desire; she has within her the extreme possibility for metamorphosis, and absolute change in her whole system of relations." This change comes in her relationship with Leon, which occurs near the end of the novel. Numen is so much within her that she is able to rule and to dominate Leon.

She sees at once that Leon is now capable of playing a part, and that to play a part is now the one thing left for herself. It is what is left for life.

Where her great attractive force has been the candor in her that could be corrupted, it is now the image-idol she can raise out of herself that has the power to corrupt. But it is not a reversal of roles; she is not to play Rodolphe; it is rather an extension of her own role from the true to the corrupt . . . she puts into Leon a degree of being which is not his but hers. She has, therefore, to force response to become attack, temptation to become corruption, suppleness to become agony, submission to become excruciation. Yet the vitality of her shamelessness is what remains in it of shame. Her behavior is excessive hysterical, habitual. She has held nothing back except what she could not give: that irreducible part of herself which does the giving because it needs it to make life supportable. Emma cannot become libertine like Rodolphe precisely because she cannot hold anything back. Rodolphe pays his bills with money and boredom and pomade, using almost nothing of himself. Emma uses money and boredom and luxury but only that she pay more fully with herself. With her, the limit is the optimum. Leon can be for us nothing more than a receptacle into which Emma pours her created self. As Emma who thought to find herself in him discovers, as a reservoir he is nothing. He acts upon Emma less as an individual than as a focus in which her passion combats the forces of society and is beaten.

And, like Anna, Emma also commits suicide.

Blackmur does not mean that Emma's corruption stems from her adultery; rather it stems from what he calls her excessive, hysterical behavior. The manner in which Numen is manifested in her is not controlled. In other words, as was the case with Anna Karenina, there is no formal regulation of Numen and as a consequence it flows irrationally and unchecked. It is one of the cardinal rules of Blackmur's critical philosophy that the life-force must be controlled by the forms of personal and collective behavior in order that it may be meaningful and useful to the individual and to society. It is interesting to remember here that Blackmur's objection to Cummings's poetry centered on just this point—that no man is ever sufficient in terms of himself. Again, the symbiotic relationship between man and his society is a necessary relationship, so that to negate social forms whether in rational discourse, social behavior, or in writing poetry is to negate a necessary source of meaning in the world. Sometimes to revitalize the self a negation of forms is necessary, as was the case with Anna and with Emma; but when this is done, new forms must be created or developed to "house" the force of Numen.

III   Ulysses

In his critiques of *Anna Karenina* and *Madame Bovary*, Blackmur was interested primarily in the human situation of the main characters as they responded to Numen. In his review of James Joyce's *Ulysses*, Blackmur focuses on Joyce's reaction to Numen and the consequence of that reaction as manifested in the structure of *Ulysses*. In other words, he is changing his focus from the characters in the novels to the human and cultural circumstances of the artist.

Blackmur begins the essay with a review of the modern cultural situation of the artist. "Is it inevitable," he asks, "that the field of reference of the most responsible authors of our time should be largely unavailable to the most responsive existing audiences? Is it unavoidable that the area of conviction and belief that lies between such author and such audience should seem rather an area of the indifferent or the provisional? Is it necessary that the guidebook to the puzzle should replace the elan of reading?" The old Greco-Christian forms of culture which artists and their audiences once shared are in decline and we are in an interim period, Blackmur believes, like that between the time of Augustus and Augustine.

The Augustinian jump took eight centuries to recover consciousness; no doubt we move faster, certainly we feel the motion to the point of vertigo, which is, socially, the characteristic feeling of an interregnum, of motion through a gap, what the old religionists call the fall into the abyss or a doomed experiment toward a secular world. Whatever the outcome, it will remain interesting to know what the jump was from and what it was that was metamorphosed; it was exactly the springboard that moved us and our present propulsive energy; and our masterpieces, being reactions willy-nilly to their time cannot help telling us, and beyond rather than merely within their intent. It is indeed their function; and it is to make use of that function that makes the best reason for getting into full relation with a given masterpiece: we can see what operations it performs upon its society. The *Ulysses* of James Joyce is a wonderfully promising example to tackle in that way.

Blackmur is again saying that the old cultural forms have broken down; new ones have not yet taken their place, and the consequence to the artist is that he has had to create his own.

The consequence to the audiences of the modern novel is that
the artist and his art have become increasingly inaccessible in
that it is difficult to understand the authors' use of the medium;
and, further, it is difficult for the audience to understand
emotionally the new artistic forms because they have not been
created out of a shared cultural experience but rather out of the
private experience of the artist. Nevertheless, Blackmur maintains, the artists and novelists must continue to create new forms
of culture, and *Ulysses* is in this sense a "rival creation."

Faced with the necessity to create his own form for his
perception of Numen, or, in other words, faced with the human
need to create order out of the chaos of his experience, Joyce
creates, Blackmur says,

a kind of nihilism of unreasonable order. He had an overmastering
predilection for order and a cultivated knowledge of many kinds of
order, and their heresies, within the Greco-Christian tradition,
catholic, classical, historical, and aesthetic, but he had to treat them all,
in fact, as if they were aesthetic, images or stresses rather than
summaries or concepts of the actual. Thus the waywardness of high
jinks in the book is order pushed, the chaos is order mixed, the disgust is
order humiliated, the exile is order desiderated or invoked. Thus, too,
the overt orders of the book—homeric, organic, stylistic—make obstacles, provoke challenges, not all of which are overcome. . . . Precisely
because Joyce could not assent to the official version of his Dublin-
classical-Christianity, he was all the more condemned to the damnation
of imposed orders. Imposed order—forced order—always mutilates
what is ordered and tends to aridify it.

As did Henry Adams, Joyce sought to impose an intellectual
order on his experience when the order called for was "in terms
of the governing concepts of those imaginations which are not
aesthetic," Blackmur writes. These are the moral and metaphysical imaginations which Joyce's

experience of his society did not provide; his only providence was the
gratuitous one of the whole undistributed flux of sensation and
possibility; and into this, every order he chose to use poured willy-
nilly. . . . Joyce had none of that conviction which is the inward sense
of outward mastery; and those who feel the lack of that sort of
conviction tend to truncate their merely outward skills: truncate,
mutilate, and mock.

In *Ulysses,* Stephen, Bloom, and Molly are manifestations of Numen. Blackmur sees Stephen as emblematic of the old Christian cultural forms which are dead. "Stephen belongs to the formalism that destroys . . . Stephen is *non serviam.* . . . Stephen is the detestable blasphemy the world creates, always inadequate to his own intent." Stephen is looking for Numen in the cultural form (religion) where it once was but is no longer. Bloom, on the other hand, because he is a Jew and nominally outside Greco-Christian culture, has a better chance to discover new sources of Numen in new personal experiences that may someday "bloom" forth into new cultural forms of a post-Christian heritage. He is the ordering intellect and Molly, his wife, represents the flowing Numen which, when joined with intellect, will produce satisfying and lasting cultural forms. But the whole novel should be seen, Blackmur says, as actually the

picture of Joyce, working out the polarities of his nature in terms of the breakdown of the Christian world as he actually experienced it in his youth. What survives even the blasphemy of thwarted faith is the double figure of Stephen, the inalienable individual, and Bloom, the inalienable Jew; survives, for Joyce, with so acute a sense of loss and inadequacy, that he had to turn to Molly—the mystery itself coarsened but still lyric—in the end. The actuality was all that the artist could give. It is up to the "other" imaginations—not the artistic, not the critical—to redeem that faith; to resume it, rather, on some new impulse of the old energy, with the realization that what was called the Church, like what was called the Crown, were temporary and temporal, were almost merely expedient, forms of the energy of man himself.

IV   The Magic Mountain

If the old Greco-Christian forms of human behavior have declined, other forms are vying to take their place. "We create," Blackmur says, "only what we potentially are. Creation is discovery." For Blackmur, the novels of Thomas Mann were creations of new forms for human behavior. "Mann's vision is gloomy: of an illness so uncopeable that it must somehow be identified with life: the vision of a society composed at every articulate point, of outsiders to that society. The gravity of our disorder seems plain," Blackmur continues, in the fact that we do not think the heroism of the outsider or of the artist unnatural, but in the right course of things. Thus we resort to private force as if it were evangelical; to private absolutisms as if they were magnanimous; to panaceas as if they were specific. This is our own form of the suicidal shame which overcame the world of the magic mountain, and which Hans Castorp, though he could not handle it, could in the end see straight, see through, and reject. It was not his disease after all, this shame on the surface convulsion—of the Blue Peter and the Silent Sister—but a deep parallel to it, at the very bottom of the anonymous and the communal.

In *The Magic Mountain*, Hans Castorp is a representative of one of the new forms of human behavior.

He is bourgeois, but he is haut-bourgeois, that is to say, the lever but not the substance of the characteristic phase human power took in the nineteenth century. . . . Mann puts it that he is mediocre, but in an honourable sense. He is a man disinclined to active life or any function of it. Trained as an engineer, he can feel no calling in it, and cannot open his great textbook on steamships. . . . He is something of an artist, but only in the sentimental sense where talent is not an issue; he neither takes nor gives authority in his relations to the arts, but bemuses them to his own less-than-conscious purposes. In short, he is representative rather than conscious of the weaknesses of the age he feels so little a part of.

It is a bourgeois age Hans Castorp belongs to and he is a representative bourgeois in a spiritually intolerable culture in which Numen is embodied in forms harmful to the human spirit. Castorp's journey to the tubercular sanitarium (the magic mountain) in the Alps is ostensibly for a two-week stay to visit his cousin, but the stay lasts for seven years. "The chief conceptual form of Mann's novel," Blackmur writes, "is the relation of Hans Castorp and his experience, and the relation is predicated more or less equally by the simplicity of Hans at an intellectual level and by the equivocalness of the experience at the level at which it is felt." Hans's intellectual simplicity assures the fact that he will respond to his experience directly, without, Blackmur tells us, substituting a conventional response for the natural one. The novel, then, is composed of a series of exposures to Numen in its older cultural forms and to Numen in its nearly pure state in the person of Peeperkorn. In fact, all the people in this novel represent one cultural form or another.

In Joachim Ziemssen, Hans' sick cousin, there is one remnant of the old world, the soldier's avowal of glory in death. . . . In Behrens, the medical director, there is the uncertainty and the humor of the question whether the disease comes to the mountain or the mountain makes the disease. In Krokowski, the psychiatrist, there is half a charlatan, but the other half is force of darkness in light: of disease as what shines in the light. In Settembrini, the humanist, there is half pretense and wayward emotion in the masquerade of order . . . but the other half is the force of aspiring rational will. In Madame Chauchat there is a tainted place—the taint of a cat always half in heat—but she is also what is tainted, or at least the sentiment of it: the vitality of the other thing, possibly shameful but in essence the very thing Settembrini would dignify if he had in reality the power he strove so feverishly to represent.

In Naphta, the Jew turned Jesuit, there is Moha as absolute will.

It is in the confrontation between Settembrini and Naphta as representatives of Numen and Moha that Blackmur sees the crucial cultural dilemna of the twentieth century. Hans continues

listening to argument after argument between the rational humanist position and the super-rational absolutist position. The one sees life philanthropically, the other sees life as a disease; they push into each other, and bind, like the dovetail joints of a box, until their friction is maximum. It makes little difference where the arguments take off, the result is the same. The crucial argument, for example, starts over capital punishment, and ends up with the will behaving like reason, and reason asserting itself wilfully. The argument has reached the merging point where nobody knows who is devout and who free-thinker. Mann's imagination is right. Surely the rational humanist is devout. Surely the Jesuit who will sacrifice everything to blessedness is a free-thinker. Surely he who would build a tolerable universe at any cost is a free-thinker and blasphemes God with the degraded remnants of his faith.

The cultural dilemma is this: if one lives by reason alone as Settembrini said he did, or by divine guidance as Naphta declared, then the forms—the manners—that are created by either reason or providence tend to be absolute and therefore one-sided. These forms raised to the level of tradition would either be "the savage absolutism of the rational truth as moral law: absolute spirit or absolute man."

There is a middle ground between reason (Numen) and providence through which the flow of Numen is unhindered yet effectively channeled into spiritually satisfying forms of behavior. This middle ground is dramatically presented in Hans's dream in the snow where he considers first giving up his life to the superior force of Nature and then considers a life in pastoral harmony "full of sweetness and light and ceremony and maternity," until "two hags dismember and devour a child . . . and he wakes, wrapped in the cold whispered brawling of their curse upon him, lying in the snow." From this dream Hans derives the insight of the middle ground and it is the combination of reason with faith and logic with belief.

He has known reason and recklessness, all of man—flesh, blood, disease, death—and knows the name for all: the human being, the delicate child of life. He knows that behind enlightened man lies the blood sacrifice; and he knows that this is better than the penny-pie of reason or the *guazzobuglio* of God and the Devil. He sees that if man can keep a little clear in the head and keep pious in the heart, then disease, health, spirit, nature are not themselves problems.

But Hans forgets his dream when he encounters Peeperkorn, who is Numen barely controlled and near the surface. Peeperkorn

is the pitch of life as force, force as fever—the pitch of life force—of going-on-ness without some presence of which, some shifting stage of which, we should all stop; but it is a force converted too far beyond the human phase—even though it is what humans are made of. So converted, it is destructive force; in serving it we are destroyed by it if we do not protect ourselves from it, just as Peeperkorn, when love and alcohol fail him, destroys himself.

Peeperkorn is also symbolic of that form of human behavior that is finishing off the last vestiges of the old cultural forms. He is symbolic of the war that interrupts the life of the inhabitants of the magic mountain. But in Hans's dream which for him is his creative effort, there are possibilities for new forms of human behavior.

V   The Brothers Karamazov

This novel was a particular favorite of Blackmur's, and he made it the subject of the last three essays in *Eleven Essays on the European Novel.* His interest lay in Dostoevski's dissection of the social soul of Russia and in his attempt to create a new "theoretic form of life" out of the old religious experience.

"Dostoevski," Blackmur says, "is so far the only writer of the first class who has attempted to dramatize the religious experience in this world and within the frame of the human psyche." Through his investigations into the religious experience Dostoevski is actually seeking to determine the relationship of institutions to human life. Why is it that forms once alive and expressive of human experience become moribund? And why is is that the old forms invariably become instruments of oppression? The brothers, Blackmur writes, are represented by the symbrms reservoir of motive—a welling pool—to dip into; and there has also been developed a high possibility of available convertibility, of likely reversibility. The old man and his sons all have the potential of reversing without altering their roles—whatever those roles may be. Even Aloysha rests on the base of sensuality; he is not yet *low* enough—squashed enough—for a monk, let alone a saint; and as for the old father, his buffoonery is the very teeter of reversibility.

The roles the characters play, their manners of behavior, are very close to the formlessness of Moha and Numen; that is, at the level where forms are created and before they become the elaborate emotional and intellectual constructs they will become, there is the primal experience of Moha and Numen differentiated only as an emotional and as an intellectual experience. At this primal experiential level, Blackmur is saying, the two kinds of base-level human experience can coalesce and the one become the other. Thus the sensuality of Dimitri's experience can suddenly become intellectual, as it does at his trial; or Aloysha's intellectual orientation can be reoriented toward sensuality. At the primal level these experiences of Numen and Moha are tremendously invigorating and the people who tend to live very near this level, like all the Karamazovs, also seem to have a charismatic quality about them.

Dostoevski is interested in discovering why the primal experience of Numen and Moha becomes rigidified in its more elaborate cultural forms. The scene that most clearly points out this theme is the meeting between Aloysha and Ivan where Ivan recounts his dream of the Grand Inquisitor. The primal experience involved here is love—or that half-sensual, half-

intellectual *sensation* that becomes the formal construct known
as love. In Ivan's dream Christ returns to sixteenth-century Spain
and is recognized and greeted by the people. The representative
of the institutional Church, the Inquisitor, has Christ thrown into
prison, where he accuses him of having rejected miracle,
mystery, and authority in favor of love and freedom as the forms
for creating meaning and happiness in human experience.
Actually, the Inquisitor and Christ represent two kinds of love—
love which is manifested in the form of power through
institutional manipulation of human behavior, and love which is
manifested in the freedom to choose one's own destiny. Christ's
love, which must constantly be renewed, allows man to create his
own forms of Numen in pursuit of happiness; the Inquisitor's
love, which does not have to be constantly renewed because it
has a social and outer framework rather than a private and inner
framework, takes account of man's inability to create new forms
of behavior to revitalize himself and therefore provides him with
an emotional and intellectual framework. It is the Inquisitor's
form of love, love that is power because it coerces and conforms
man into a framework, that becomes spiritually stultifying and
deadening to the individual. And why, in Blackmur's view, does
this happen? All forms of Numen become lifeless, he says, when
they become an "affront to man's nature"; the individual
disappears in the form when the form does not correspond to
what the individual would have created for himself given the
chance. Thus Ivan's, Aloysha's, Dimitri's, as well as Anna's and
Emma's human situation is the same—the forms no longer fit. In
The Brothers Karamozov everyone "is on the edge of a new life
or a fresh start. The patterns are about to cross, the patterns of
the fictions we tell in which we find life tolerable. Aloysha is at
the critical moment of his early experience when the kind of
fictions he will make will be determined. It is good to think of
man's psyche as the music to which he sets himself, whether he—
or we—know his fictions or not."

If one is about to make a new start the crucial question then
becomes, as it did in Anna Karenina's situation, how is one to
respond to Numen? When one is in rebellion against the
established forms of human behavior, how does one respond to
Numen in such a way that new behavior patterns can be
established? In *The Brothers Karamazov* this is the question that
Dostoevski asks in the episode of Dimitri's trial. Rebellion

against the accepted forms of human behavior is the real crime for which Dimitri is tried. "Dimitri speaks the truth," Blackmur mentions, "because of which he wishes to die honest, with which he must deal: forces which are in the conditions of life. What Dimitri stands for here is the plea that conditions are not ends, nor beginnings, nor meanings. A man does not need positive aspirations or ideals to be revolted at the conditions in which he finds himself; he will respond by tragic gestures and comfort himself by crying out in the most revolting conditions of all." Dimitri's whole response to society is irresponsible, so he is convicted by the peasants of having murdered his father. Yet throughout the trial Dimitri is continually able to envision a new life and in that ability lies the solution to the question. Dimitri has the imagination to stay in contact with reality, with Numen. His imagination needs to be supplemented and leavened with reason, however, so that the new forms of behavior he creates are responsible to and compatible with a new society established on the basis of those new forms. One responds to Numen, Blackmur believes, with imagination and with reason in a "great act of will, capable of uniting in a single responsive act the two forms of responsibility—to the possibilities and to the everlasting necessities of life."

VI   *Conclusion*

In his criticism of literature, Blackmur took on the most difficult critical task of all in trying to interpret not only the novel itself but also its relationship to and function within the Western cultural heritage. In his criticism of literature, he set out to do what he said the critic in our time must do—build bridges between society and the arts. Literature—novels—were his special concern but he meant his bridges for all the arts. He perceived that we are so hopelessly confused in our understanding of our culture that we need the critic, the master-layman, to set us straight.

The critical structure he set forth was intended to handle the novel's relationship to and function within the Western heritage. It is a simple structure, really, but it has the passion and force of a new belief, a new religion with its forces of light and dark, good and evil, Numen and Moha. The structure fulfills one of the primary criteria of any critical scheme—that it enhance our understanding of literature. But Blackmur's critical structure goes beyond and enhances our understanding of ourselves and of our time. By incorporating metaphysical and ethical concerns, Blackmur's critical framework puts our lives into perspective and intimately involves us in the creation of meaning and sense in a disordered and inane world. We are given an explanation of our spiritual poverty and why it is we reject our institutions as lifeless. We are also shown the light and what we must do to gain the light. This is criticism as philosophy, or criticism raised to a plane where it functions as philosophy.

CHAPTER 6

Creative Criticism

I *Reason In Madness*

B LACKMUR's four Library of Congress lectures given in 1956
are typical of the impressionistic style of his later essays.
They are critical poems in which he embodied the major themes
and insights of his career in letters. They are synoptic, aphoristic,
suggestive, intense, and they follow in the tradition of William
Hazlitt and Walter Pater, who undertook to formulate verbal
equivalents of the aesthetic effects of the works they criticized.
Instead of giving an impressionistic account of a single work or
group of works, Blackmur, in his Library of Congress lectures,
attempted to formulate the verbal equivalent of his own
response to Western culture. These lectures represent Blackmur's highest critical achievement because the creative impulse
behind them came not from an instance of literature but from his
perception of and from his imaginative recreation of his culture
and society. These critical essays, then, had the same genesis as a
novel and, Blackmur hoped, would have the same aesthetic
effect.

To begin, Blackmur assumes that we spend our lives seeking
some meaningful pattern—reason in madness. The individual's
reason creates order and without reason there can be no order,
no recognition of the facts of experience. "Reason" he says, "is in
substance all the living memory of the mind; in action (or, if you
like, in essence) reason is the recognition and creation of order
where disorder was."[1] The central spiritual problem of the
twentieth century, Blackmur says, is that society and particularly
the arts have lost their ability to create order. The consequence
is disorder in society and in the arts, which in turn has spun off
new "troubles." By "Disorder" Blackmur means the absence of a
pattern that gives life meaning. And pattern here means the

artist's attitude toward life. The troubles he refers to are a "combination of turbulence and apathy, of novelty and isolation, immersed in the new failures of human relationships." In addition Blackmur believes that we have so fragmented and specialized our knowledge that we are unable to create order through what we know. He quotes Arnold Toynbee's words that "our Western scientific knowledge of which we boast, and even our Western technique for turning this knowledge to practical account—a technique upon which we depend for our wealth and strength—is seriously esoteric."[2] Not only is our scientific knowledge "seriously esoteric," but also the "new knowledges" of psychology, anthropology, sociology, and psychiatry are fragmented and specialized to the point where instead of supplying techniques for insight into the human experience, they have become

techniques for finding—even creating—trouble: new ways of under-mining personality and conviction and belief and human relation. We have psychology which dissolves the personality into bad behavior, we have anthropology which dissolves religion into a competition, world-and history-wide, of monsters, and we have psychiatry which cures the disease by making a monument of it and sociology which flattens us into the average of the lonely crowd. We have thus the tools with which to construct the age of anxiety out of the older debris.[3]

These new knowledges, Blackmur believes, have become "techniques of trouble" used not for the perception and understanding of human experience but for the manipulation of individuals. Moreover, these techniques of trouble have extended "along new lines the malicious criticism of knowledge (the attack on the validity of perception). . . . All the apprehensive powers of the mind have been put at such a discount that they are felt to be irrational, when actually they are the fountainhead and fountain reach of reason herself." "It strikes me here," Blackmur goes on to say,

that in result upon our general mind, modern physics and mathematics make a parallel extension of the same malicious criticism of knowledge: as refinement of critical abstraction, good for manipulation, rotten for apprehension—that is, for the sensual knowledge that is the immediate rock of physics and the thing indexed by mathematics. As compared to literary criticism, the critique supplied by physics is both more malice and more knowledge and is also more remote from the apprehending reason. The effect of these malicious critiques is profound: almost they dissolve our sense of the texture of moral experience. It is the writhing of actual knowledge under these malicious techniques that makes choice and purpose and taste so difficult, uncertain, and fractious.[4]

There are two points in the previous passage worth emphasizing. The first is that Blackmur believes that the new knowledges create statistical abstractions out of "real" experience so that it is impossible for reason to make such abstracted experience intelligible. I assume that Blackmur is thinking of the layman, not the expert, although since the expert cannot be expert in everything, he too at some time must face bewildering statistical abstractions. Further, abstracted experience is less immediate, less affective. The meaning or knowledge reason derives from statistical abstractions is less "sensual" than knowledge derived from immediately apprehended experience.

The second point is that Blackmur believes that the new knowledges are mounting an increasingly effective attack on the confidence of individuals in the apprehensive powers of their minds. The experts are undermining the layman's confidence in his ability to perceive reality. The overall effect of the new knowledges or techniques of trouble has been to undermine reason and to add to disorder.

If the new knowledges have contributed to the decline of the efficacy of reason, so has the decline of what Blackmur calls "bourgeois humanism." "Bourgeois humanism (the treasure of residual reason in live relation to the madness of the senses) is the only conscious art of the mind designed to deal with our megalopolitan mass society: it alone knows what *to do with* momentum in its new guise; and it alone knows that it must be more than itself without losing itself in order to succeed."[5] Bourgeois humanism is a skill that in the past, Blackmur says, had been taught to society by her artists. It is the skill of apperception or the ability to understand present experience in terms of past experience. To Blackmur, this skill is one of the best ways of creating order. Unfortunately, "The decay of the prestige of bourgeois humanism was perhaps necessary, but only as an interim, a condition of interregnum, when new forces overran us." In other words, there had to be a decline in the prestige of the older order (bourgeois humanism) before new achievements in the arts could be possible. But the loss of prestige leaves a vacuum which must somehow be filled by a new order or by an older order with new prestige. As was pointed out in Chapter 2, Blackmur's main interest in the poetry of Yeats and Eliot was in the concept of order each adopted as a guiding principle for his poetry. Both poets chose older concepts of order—Yeats chose magic, Eliot chose Christianity—in attempting to fill the void created by the decline in bourgeois humanism.

Blackmur expected that the arts would develop some new concept of order that would replace bourgeois humanism. "Instead," he says, "we have the apparition of the arts asserting their authority in a combination of the spontaneous and the arbitrary, in pure poetry and pure expression and pure trouble. Instead of creation in honesty, we have assertion in desperation; we have a fanaticism of the accidental instead of growth of will."[6] This is the same idea behind his dislike of Cummings's poetry. "The anarchy of our artists," he continues, "is in response to facts as well as in evasion of facts. The two great external facts of our time are the explosion of populations and the explosions of the new energies. The two great internal facts of our time are the recreation of the devil (or pure behavior) in a place of authority and the development of techniques for finding destructive troubles in the psyche of individuals." To understand what Blackmur means by "the recreation of the devil in place of authority," we must review his understanding of expressionism. In the first place, he believes that art creates a world, a reality, that is a "rival creation" to the actual reality the artist perceives. He maintains that there must be order in this rival creation which requires reason to create the order. However, he says, because we live in an expressionistic age, "Instead of rationalizing our experience we give our experience what form we can and set reason new and almost impossible tasks to perform." According to Blackmur, expressionism does not create a rival world through reason because it is an attempt to transmute feeling directly into art. Without reason in the transmutation process, the result of the artist's efforts amounts to little more than an idiosyncratic expression difficult to understand. In addition, expressionism's rival creation is really a piece of the actual; that is, it merely reflects reality without changing it or creating a new order out of it in accordance with some principle. Therefore, expressionistic art reflects unchanged what Blackmur calls the devil or the demonic forces in modern society. "The devil," he says,

always takes the form of the actual most conspicuously in an expressionistic age. Expressionism—what I say is both myself in truth and creates a new world—tends to pyrotechnics; the fireworks are within us and are all around us and are their own meaning—subject to the least possible external control or common predictable forms of understanding. In expressionistic art we see what the forces are which we have to control by other means: the actual forces of human nature, or nonrational behavior, and of the industriously rational machinations of the devil—the diabolic, the demonic, and the chthonic—the life that is in our soil.[7]

The forces we have to control by other means make up disorder—there is no pattern in those forces and therefore reason must create one. And the history of twentieth-century art is the history of successful and unsuccessful attempts at the creation of order. As described in the previous chapter, the forces of human nature Blackmur terms Moha, and the other forces of culture and its institutions are permeated by the life-force, the Numen which also flows and mingles with the Moha. And between them, between the Numen and the Moha, is art. Expressionism, however, expresses human nature directly—express Moha directly—without the leavening of Numen in forms constructed by reason.

So far Blackmur has given us the same general critique of culture that he gave us in his criticism of the European novel. Man is adrift without spiritual beacons of light and he must therefore find his own harbors. But Blackmur is not content with the Romantic expressionism that is the result of every man for himself. If every man, every artist, is to create his own meaning in life, this will result in a greater alienation than now exists. What is the solution? To Blackmur, the solution lies in the creation of mutually understandable forms of meaning or order. If the individual creations of order were reasonable; that is, if they could be understood by others, then a society, a new culture, could be generated through that mutual understanding. Meaning in life was for him a function of reason and any art or profession which created human confusion rather than human understanding was anathema. To him also, the new professions of the twentieth century—psychiatry and sociology and the like—

created more confusion than understanding because they used reason in the wrong way. They used it as a number counter or as a statistical abstractor, and instead of recognizing their mistake, men in the new professions seemed to Blackmur to be perversely compounding it. He could explain this continuing state of affairs only by invoking the devil or the concept of the demonic. And he felt that the only way to get rid of the devil was by exorcising him through reason used sensuously—that is, reason used in intimate conjunction with the sensual perception of experience.

Because he knew most about literature, he illustrated his thoughts by referring to literary movements and to individual artists as being emblematic of the spiritual difficulty of living in an expressionistic age. The artists of the Dada movement, for instance, rejected any attempt at creating order. "In the eyes of these men 'everything had already been torn down; dadaism could be only an inventory of the ruins, and a declaration of the failure, or more accurately, the death of a civilization.' "[8] The dadaists, Blackmur continues, "prevented masterpieces at all costs," and rejected tradition. By denying reason they made it impossible for themselves to understand their own situation.

Virginia Woolf, on the other hand, lost herself in Romantic expressionism and therefore lost contact with her fellow humans. "In Virginia Woolf," Blackmur says, "human relations disappear in the very technique of sensibility in which they were supposed to be lodged and understood. . . . In Virginia Woolf's world there is no possible society or daily life . . . both the voices and the flesh are separated from us, and staled [made less vivid or real], by the intermission of woolen curtains through which nothing is touched; and Mrs. Woolf in her diary could not understand what all the bother over *Ulysses* was about."[9]

Similarly, in the poetry of D. H. Lawrence "the hysteria of direct sensual experience destroys every structure of sensibility, and there is only as much human relation as there is possible in the swoon of the blood, which is a very powerful and very destructive relation indeed."[10] This is the same criticism in almost the same words that Blackmur had for Lawrence's poetry twenty-five years earlier. The meaning Lawrence makes out of his experience is a private one in that it cannot be understood rationally, although it may be understood emotionally.

William Faulkner and Marcel Proust are also victims of their expressionistic designs of order. "Let us think of Faulkner," Blackmur writes,

and ask of him why it is that he has deliberately surrendered the advantages of syntax without establishing any comparable control over the movements of his beautiful prose. Why has he left the harmony out at the level of notation, at the level where the reader is instructed how to read? It is precisely what the reader cannot be trusted to put in. In his books, the words, if not the people, fall out of relation; indeed the words heap round the people and obscure them—quite as if Faulkner used the words for which he has in fact an overwhelming gift only because on the printed page he could not do without them.[11]

Any denial or apparent nonuse of a form of order bothers Blackmur. He is not being petty when he objects to Faulkner's apparent inattention to the rules of syntax; rather, he is objecting on principle to any negation of order.

Blackmur praises Proust's intelligence but also cites it as the source of the difficulty in his writing.

Though Proust thought of himself as an anti-intellectual, it was so that he could keep himself from the fixed intellect and the formalized point of view; he maintained intelligence at the pitch where it refuses action; he preferred transmutations to action, the shifting of the phases of the heart to the phases of the reason, both somehow attached to the deep viscous memory, of which the heart and the reason are two decimations. May we not say, then, that Proust and Faulkner at bottom both suffer from absence of syntax, the power of composing or arranging things, giving them ordinance, so that their parts are in living relation to the intelligence? Faulkner runs to the syntax of analogous action; Proust runs rather to the syntax of words and intelligence and only seldom engages them in the autonomy of dramatic action.[12]

In Blackmur's view, neither Faulkner nor Proust practiced the literary techniques required to deal with disorder because neither had the power to arrange and compose their experience so that it related to the general experience of their cultures as Dante's *Divine Comedy* related to and depended on twelfth-century Christianity. The order Blackmur has in mind is a metaphysical order in which man is able to define his nature and to establish his relationships with other men. The conceptual framework of the art work must either "fit" this kind of order as

Dante's did or embody it as a rival creation to the old forms of order. This places an enormous burden on the artist to be both artist and metaphysician. Faulkner and Proust fail to be metaphysicians. Faulkner's order, Blackmur says, is the order of actions, that is, the order of human behavior or the order of Moha; there is no relation to the general human condition. Proust's order is the order of the unengaged intelligence; the order also does not relate to the world.

Since Blackmur is offering his own rival creation in these Library of Congress lectures, he must be a metaphysician himself if he is to follow his own criterion. That is, he must offer his own concept of the nature of man. Before he does that, however, he wants to make clear why certain individual conceptions of man in the twentieth century have failed. In the work of Luigi Pirandello, for instance, there is a failure to create a form for human identity. Pirandello's work suggests

the kind of movement and the kind of withdrawal the psyche makes in its craving for that form which determines identity. It is almost a biological form and is rather like an amoeba (a figure which for this context I borrow from Francis Fergusson speaking of the psyche in Dante)—an amoeba which takes form and color and shifting contour— indeed takes its detours—from the forces which attract it or which touch it. In Pirandello the self is adaptable by contagion and by desire and by thought, and both to itself and to others. The self is dramatically creative in all the roles it assumes, but remains—whence its suffering and its joys—through all its phases vitally itself, its own identity, something as diaphanous, as individual, and as humorous as an ever-fresh voice. This, if you like, is the *play* of modern psychology by which the personality achieves itself. To read the novels and stories, to read or to see the plays of Pirandello leads all the amoeba in oneself to take on the successive adventures of being. In Pirandello, the principle within fastens itself onto all the possibilities from without.[13]

Pirandello never answers the question of what it is to be human because he offers too many possibilities.

If Pirandello expands the possibilities of human identity, Franz Kafka, on the other hand, reduces them. Kafka defines the human in terms of guilt and isolation. "In Kafka you find your identity in your guilt, you find it in an alien and official world . . . you find it only when you have been excluded and turn yourself in absolute isolation. . . . It is a world where to achieve identity there is a logical reduction of possibility. . . ."[14] In addition,

Blackmur goes on to say, Kafka had "a terrible vision of all within us that is against ourselves; he did not destroy, but he inverted his bourgeois humanism; precisely as Pirandello, as all but the worst Italians do, began afresh with what made humanism worthwhile." Kafka's vision of human nature fails because it does not expand the human possibilities, it is too limiting. It should be pointed out that by the term "fail" Blackmur does not mean artistic failure so much as a failure to produce a satisfying metaphysical description of human nature and human possibility.

Blackmur balances off his discussion of failed metaphysical descriptions with a discussion of some that he thinks are satisfying to the human spirit. In the works of the writers previously discussed, Blackmur says, "we saw fragments of the troubles that are, forms from the techniques of new troubles our age has discovered, and attempts, greater or less, to encompass and to cope with these troubles with the technical resources of humane imagination; with whatever had survived in the gift of each author of bourgeois humanism."[15] That is, the artists had to construct order using bits and pieces of the old order identified as Greco-Christian. And their audience had to bring to the works produced, Blackmur says, "something which was our own and not specifically called for; we had to bring what was not there and needed. Like ourselves, the work of these writers was incomplete."[16] The key word here is "incomplete." None of the previously discussed writers had a complete vision of order, or what Blackmur calls a "systematic metaphysics that bears on daily life."[17] These writers did not offer in their work a description of human nature that was complete nor did they offer a pattern for human experience. The reader had to bring to the works in question his own metaphysics and his own patterns. But this is asking too much of a twentieth-century audience that has lost the power of symbolic thinking and, more importantly, the sense of a shared human experience. It is up to the artists, Blackmur believes, to offer complete "rival creations" in which the readers, the audience, may find meaning and order for their lives.

II *Rival Creations*

Three writers who, in Blackmur's view offer complete rival creations are Thomas Mann, André Gide, and James Joyce. These three require us to bring a great deal, and more than our other writers, but who specify in the very nature of their work what is is that we must bring; and precisely because they are writers whose work is more nearly complete and cannot easily be exhausted; work which because of its formal superiority, supplied with tact and skill by the authors, goes on if not to new life at least to new and different uses, and which as much as any of the rival creations of the mere mind has a life of its own, a life which consists precisely in having given shape and theoretic form to our troubles.[18]

Instead of bringing his own metaphysic and his own patterns of life to the work, the reader of these writers need only bring an "openness" or willingness to understand the theoretic forms they give to life. Mann, Gide, and Joyce made "great forms, and it was by their forms that they aroused antagonism and commanded assent; and they demanded attention, which they often got, beyond the habits of the amused part of the mind at this or in any other time. Let us see how this was done."[19]

The great theoretic form in the work of Thomas Mann is called bourgeois humanism by Blackmur. The order of experience which Mann gives to his characters make them, Blackmur says, "bourgeois humanists tainted by art."

It is the taint of the artist in them that raises them to heroic proportions; for it is that which compels them to take stock of the sick and ailing, to seize on the unseemly, to expect the equivocal, and to rejoice in the problematic. These heroes are the outsiders within and participating in their society. They are all demonic people redeemed from the diabolic by the human, but they would not have been demonic had they not gone in for all the unseeing, all the lowgrade relations we have in human nature. . . . Almost one says that these heroes are great, in their different ways, by reason of their infatuation. Almost but not quite; for they are all gifted and skilled with the other lust which is the humanistic lust for knowledge, till knowledge itself seems a degradation of being or another taint in the soul, and truth becomes a kind of fiction—a kind of vital fraud practiced by the artist on his humane knowledge out of his total irresponsibility.[20]

Mann has managed to include in his theoretic form of bourgeois humanism the base-level human experience of Numen and Moha and the struggle to fit this experience into behavioral patterns consistent with the possibilities of human development.

André Gide's theoretic form is the moral life lived in constant proximity to temptation. "He is the French puritan who nurses the devil within him, not as a poor relation as in Mann and Dostoevski but in his older and prouder role as the Prince of Darkness in whose service we must perform most of our acts, since he is our feudal self."[21] In Gide's *The Counterfeiters,* the devil

migrates from character to character. In some he seizes the form of *depit*—chagrin mixed with anger, rancor, and grudge as motivation: the source of what people do against their own good in relation to others. In some he floods woe and anguish, as in Laura and in La Pérouse: the source of what people do to their own ill for the good of others or the service of truth. In some he encourages instinct when thwarted or released by wealth or frustration, as in Pasavant or Armond or Lillian. This devil always comes intending to stay; he is the prince of others' means. He has great strength of personality, great capacity for taking advantage of the situation, whatever turns up, or might turn up, and he cheats nobody so much as those who would woo him.[22]

In *Ulysses* Joyce created a theoretic form "in which we can become lost and can find ourselves, but which we cannot imitate except in him." "Joyce went at his work as Dante did," Blackmur goes on to say,

and tried to read his experience through every form or mode of knowledge available to him. The interesting thing is that he did so against the general will and custom of his time and without the aid of recognized modes for the creation and interpretation of such a reading. He had no four-fold pattern. He had to revolt against himself as well as his time and he had to use both himself and his time. He was compelled to create, as if single-handed, symbolic modes in which he could dramatize the city of man he knew. Whatever success he had came from his fundamental mastery of actual experience and his equally fundamental mastery of actual language, where each mastery was a foil and counterpart to the other.[23]

The theoretic form Joyce created is an amalgam of all the older patterns of human experience—that is why the reader can get lost in his work. But as Blackmur states, the reader cannot imitate or use this amalgam except when reading Joyce. Joyce's theoretic form is complete but not transferable. It is a conscious product— a product of reason and of imagination but not a product of the emotions.

III   *Analogical Form*

At this point Blackmur is ready to begin his explanation of his own metaphysics and to describe his own theoretic form for human experience. And he finds the sources of both in poetry. As he did in his discussion of literature, Blackmur begins his discussion of poetry with a description of the cultural situation of twentieth-century poets. Poetry has become fragmented, esoteric, and specialized; and the poet has "found himself speaking a private language and has grown proud of it."[24] Like the novelists, poets no longer feel themselves to be part of the culture and this feeling of alienation has cut them off from their natural source of inspiration. Blackmur writes:

Faced with the dissolution of thought and the isolation of the artist, faced with the new industrialization of the intellect, what else could [the poet] do but declare his independence and self-sufficient supremacy both as an intellectual and as an artist? Let us admit that the new independence came partly out of the old claims for and defenses of poetry from Aristotle through Shelley, partly from the nineteenth-century claims made by Ruskin and Arnold, all of which allied art deeply to society, but partly—and this is the biggest emotional part— from the blow of the First World War and what seemed the alienation of the artist from a society increasingly less aesthetically-minded—less interested in the vivid apprehension of the values of the individual.[25]

Because society has become "less interested in the vivid apprehension of the values of the individual," poetry has become increasingly esoteric. That is, the conventions by which, and through which, the poet expresses his apprehension of reality are not understood by the public. It has always been difficult, Blackmur says,

for the artist to find means of expressing his own direct apprehension of life in conventions which were, or could be made, part of the conventions of society in general; and this, also—this problem of communication—has become excessively difficult in a society which tends to reject the kind of faithful conventions under which the artist has usually worked, and society in which, under the urban process, and under the weight of the new knowledges, so much of thought has been given over to mechanisms which had formerly operated under faith. These are the conditions under which the artist has felt, in his exaggeration of them, isolated and has asserted himself under the general state of mind that runs from art for art's sake through surrealism to Existenz. . . .[26]

It is interesting to note that at this late stage in his career Blackmur seems to have thought that a poet like Cummings could not be totally blamed for his "sentimental denial of the intellect." Social factors partially are at fault. After all, even T. S. Eliot seemed to be creating a private idiom in his poetry of the 1920s; but the difference between Eliot and Cummings for Blackmur was that Eliot's poetry strove to "deal with" the cultural situation in a new idiom encased in a new intellectual framework of meaning that was understandable and rationally communicable while Cummings's poetry did not.

Like the novelists, then, the poets of the twentieth century have had to deal with the new troubles of isolation, alienation, and disorder. And, says Blackmur, "the poets have been led to deal with them (or to repel them, or rival them) in a kind of irregular and spasmodic, but vitalized metaphysics."[27] In this century, poets have generally tried to write poetry from "*inside the experience and outside the point of view of reason.*"[28] The consequence has been the development of a poetry that is heavily symbolic and sensual. In other words (Cummings is the example and so is Rod McKuen) poets have tried to fuse their feelings into the words they chose to express them. "*This,*" Blackmur writes,

is the disassociation of ideas, it is the fusion of senses and the exercise of their interchangeability in words and thereby thoughts and ideas, and it *is* the representative notion behind the enormous stride of sensuality in the last century of poetry—for however metaphysical or symbolical we may have become in our poetry we have also acquired for it a sensuality no modern language has hitherto known. If Rilke had his angels, Lorca had his gypsies. It is these we have put side by side, and in them seen our permanent analogies.[29]

The poetic device which symbolizes the fusion of sense with thoughts and ideas is the new theoretic form for human experience. And the name of this new form is "analogy." "Analogy is exactly the putting of things side by side. In poetry they are bound together by rhythm, sped by meter, united by vision, experienced by music, said in voice. In analogy we get the relation of attributes, not substances; we get the *form* of reality as if form were itself a kind of action. . . . Analogy is indeed the very name for our characteristic poetic logics."[30] Analogy, then, is the linking of ideas, images, feelings, emotions, reactions, smells, etc., which may have no relation to each other except in the poet's mind. Analogical form is poetic logic, and the attraction of analogical form for modern poets is due to "the fragmentation of faith and the diversity of logics and the divisiveness of our minds generally."[31] Analogical form allows poets to express disorder, alienation, and isolation by putting disparate images of each together in the same poem. But, Blackmur goes on to say, analogical form is not really a new form—medieval poets used it to explain and to interpret a unity which was "insistently present." To modern poets, "unity is what we only seek by all the machineries of desperation and longing, sometimes longing without hope; and the means of our search is by analogy or collateral form."[32]

But the problem with analogical form is that it still rests on a private logic. What images the poet puts together still depends upon an internal logic of his own. Analogical form expresses the individual poet's feeling for the relationship between disparate things. This feeling constitutes his vision of unity of experience but is by its nature a continually changing phenomenon. What is felt to be related is continually changing so that poems which express a certain feeling of the relationship between things may change, grow, or disappear according to whether this expressed relationship is psychologically satisfactory to others—in other words, whether or not the poem also expresses for them their feeling of the relatedness of disparate images.

There is a sense, Blackmur says, in which to give experience a form is to "create" it. That is, analogical form can be said to have created the modern experiences of isolation, alienation, and disorder. "It is only an exaggeration, then, to say that poetry created the morals of the modern world, and sets in action the modes of human love and all the other heroic or rebellious modes of human behavior. . . . I do not say that this is what modern poetry 'really' does, but that this is sometimes its operative ambition and its saving illusion. . . . Every new form of knowledge, or of the human, is monstrous until it is made a part of the acknowledgement of reason."[33] The analogical form of modern poetry creates modern experience in the sense that a poem is a rival creation to reality. But the form by itself means nothing until the poet's reason makes it part of the poetic and intellectual tradition of the culture. That is, analogical form must be recognized by other members of society as a viable and satisfying form of *their* experience also.

Unfortunately, modern poetry by and large has not depended upon reason or the ordering faculty of the mind. It is the first learned poetry since Milton, Blackmur writes, "With the singular difference that it is also and deliberately irrational in its processes—is indeed an effort to erode the rational for metaphysical purposes."[34] The irrational processes Blackmur refers to are illustrated in certain poems of Eliot. *The Waste Land,* for example, "requires a maxiumum of structures, and requires it in the effort to do the job of reason in the absence of effective predictive form. Reason had above all to do the labor of associating the elements of a sensibility believed to be dissoci-ated empirically. This, if you like, was reason in madness, operating and drawing from madness; it was reason controlling madness."[35] Blackmur means that the images in analogy in Eliot's poetry did not seem at first to his readers to be in meaningful relation to each other. The reader's reason, or rather, the critic's job of work, in the twentieth century was to explain the nature of the relations between images in modern poetry. The critic must establish and explain the meaning of the Sibyl-Tiresias analogy in *The Waste Land* to make an understanding of the poem possible for its readers. Otherwise, the meaning of the poem remains private. But this image is only one of many in the poem that must be explained to the reader "because there is no recognizable principle of composition." "The reason would not have been able to take up her task of poetic thought had not the psyche (one's private share of the Numen) brought in the compulsive force of images, of the obsession of dreams, and of the force of dramatic mimesis to set up and reveal the hidden analogies of things. Thus it was that those of us who knew the least in the intellectual sense, in the first instance understood the poem best."[36]

Those who responded to modern poetry with their imagina-tions understood it more clearly than those who responded with their intellects alone. In fact, the best response would have been one in which intellects and imaginations were fused. But, the fact remains, those who responded more in imaginative terms understood modern poetry better than those who did not. Why this was so, Blackmur explains, is that *The Waste Land* and modern poetry in general have for their principle of order an "irregular sensual metaphysic." The sensuality of modern poetry is now, however, an easily recognizable principle of composition because in Blackmur's view sensuality is not something that can be accounted for by reason. Like gesture, sensuality in poetry is an ineffable part of the total meaning of a poem and may be accounted for only through imagination. Again like gesture, it may be talked about in imaginative terms and accounted for critically through an analysis of the poetic structure which surrounds it.

Sensuality is the vitality of felt experience or an awareness of the Numen. Sensual poetry is poetry where the words or thoughts are felt as an experience. "In the poetry of Eros—the force from below, the impulse that satisfies itself only ,in the instance—we see emphatic cases of the experience of thought where, if you like, the experience becomes very near becoming thought—as near as symbolic action can come. This is one of the great examples of tautology: where things become their own meaning: which is the condition of poetry—however great or narrow the selection of experience may be."[37] An example of sensuality in poetry is Yeats's "Leda and the Swan." It was not "the annunciation of Greek civilization and the turning of the Great Year . . . that disturbed the churchmen of Dublin when the poem first appeared," Blackmur says; "rather, it was the staggering,. vague blow of the knowledge and power of the central, spreading, sexual quick: the loosening of thought into life and into itself, with a gained life."[38] Thought and life merge in this poem so that the *meaning* of the poem for Blackmur is his experience in reading it.

The coming together of life and thought, reason and imagination, Numen and Moha in analogical form so that what is *thought* is also sensuously felt as experience gives a clue to Blackmur's metaphysics. These Library of Congress essays were meant to be the form for the felt concept of the nature of man. Blackmur believed that man was a rational-instinctual being who could rationally understand his emotions and emotionalize his rationality. The highest state of being would be a balance, and this balance would be an emotional and spiritual fulfillment of human potential. But he also knew that man was still on his way to achieving this balance and needed the corrective of art to remind him continually of his nature and the possibilities for developing that nature into a perfectly integrated balance. Seen in this light, Blackmur's later criticism becomes art or serves the same function as art. In reading these particular essays, one is at first bewildered by the impressionistic language and the images and examples piled one on top of the other. But this is precisely analogical form, and the piling up of critical examples induces a feeling in the reader of what the writer is talking about. If the reader is bewildered and confused in reading these essays he is supposed to be, because bewilderment and confusion are part of our culture and therefore part of our art. But Blackmur doesn't want his essays to be private in the sense that they are his alone to understand. On the contrary, he expects the reader to come to an understanding *through* his feeling of confusion by eventually discovering the underlying theoretic form which is analogical. In this way these essays become their own meaning. The structure of the essays—the analogical form—is *felt* as the structure of human experience, and from this feeling Blackmur hoped would come a rational recognition of ourselves and of our momentum.

CHAPTER 7

The Poetry

BLACKMUR'S three published volumes of poetry never received the attention or the acclaim of his criticism. To a certain extent, this reflects a legitimate valuation—Blackmur was certainly a far better critic than poet. But the poetry should not be set aside, especially since to read it is to be immersed in a graceful style of intelligence.

The poems published in *From Jordan's Delight* (1937), *The Second World* (1942), and *The Good European* (1947) reflect Blackmur's critical principles. They are carefully crafted, illustrate Blackmur's wide reading, and each evidences a careful restraint and distrust of the immediately emotional. Blackmur was most successful in his short poems, where he seems to have been most comfortable. His themes were those usually found in the personal lyric: love, death, loneliness, frustration, sex, faith. But Blackmur also wrote on themes of a larger importance: war, chaos and order, the torment of nations. The thematic emphasis of the poetry tends to go in the same direction as does the critical emphasis; that is, the poetry, like the criticism, becomes progressively more preoccupied with social themes in the personal context of the artist's relationship to his society.

As one might expect, Blackmur's poems illustrate his concern for craftsmanship and his mastery of prosody. Two poems, "O Sleeping Lear" and "Threnos," are particularly fine examples of Blackmur's skill.[1] The first dates from the 1930s and is part vi of the long poem "From Jordan's Delight." The second is a late poem, written in 1960.

O Sleeping Lear

Wayward the wind weighs
For us who merely be

Westly on warm days
Eastly to rough the sea

Here wayward fishers come
Full twelve on the rock beach
To split a salvaged drum
Red rum and ruddy speech

Here come all undone
Shirt out and all askew
Slipping jarred his gun
And blood ran ruddy too

What blood was that what gale
What yelling, belling cry
What signal in wind's wail
What fading frosting eye

Wayward the wind weighs
For us who merely be
All steady north these days
And no mirage asea

The blessed man got up
From rum and lobster ran
Huge to the north cliff top
And giant there began

Heaving the island down
And heaving the boulder word
Earth clods wood red, root brown
Until he fell and snored

Who shall the sleeper mock
Who smoothe his thinning hair
O eddy of whorled rock
O eddying headlost air

THRENOS

Among the grave, the gross, the green
everlasting images are seen:
the grace of God, old girls, and March grass
How hoarse in counterpart this theme,
an allelulia also alas

See there upon full sea the still
Blossoming of Jordan's heath,
And on the change, all living ill:
O eddying, bodiless faith.

Written some thirty years apart, these two poems clearly show
evidence of Blackmur's mastery of assonance, consonance,
alliteration, and poetic form. He was most comfortable using the
four- or five-line stanza and he particularly liked masculine end
rhyme (green-seen, still-ill). His best poems are written in short
iambic or trochaic tetrameter or pentameter lines. Blackmur also
wrote his best poetry when he used imagery of the sea or of the
earth. As a man who spent his summers on the shore at
Harrington, Maine, he knew the sea, the tides, and the shoreline
well enough. The "Jordan" referred to could be both the biblical
Jordan and an island called Jordan's Delight off the mouths of
Naraguagus and Pigeon Hill Bays, eastern Maine.

Blackmur's use of the word "eddy" illustrates in an interesting
way his critical principle that "when a word is used in a poem it
should be the sum of all its appropriate history made concrete
and particular in the individual contest; and in poetry all words
act *as if* they were so used, because the only kind of meaning
poetry can have requires that all its words resume their full life:
the full life being modified and made unique by the *qualifications* the words perform one upon the other in the poem."[2] An
eddy is a current at variance with the main current in a stream of
liquid or gas and has a rotary or whirling motion. All instances of
Blackmur's use of "eddy" in the above poems may be found as
separate entries in the Oxford English Dictionary. Of particular
interest in the entry under "Eddy-wind" taken from Ward's 1647
The Simple Cobler of Agawam: . . . "Men that are weather-waft
up and down with every eddy-wind of every new doctrine." In
his criticism, Blackmur counseled against doctrinaire thought in
favor of thinking as an ongoing process. This process, which
Blackmur would characterize as saltatory, always on the move,
provisional, is the lens through which he views all his experience.
The use of the word "eddy" in each of its historic contexts is the
poetic equivalent of this process. Words, for Blackmur, are never
fixed but are "the sum of all [their] appropriate history."

Blackmur's belief in process or momentum as he called it in his criticism made for certain difficulties in his writing of poetry. T. S. Eliot wrote to Blackmur in 1926:[3]

I am returning herewith a long poem [possibly "A Funeral for a Few Sticks" (1925)] which you sent me nearly a year ago. The reason that I have kept it for so long is that I was enough interested in it to want to repay you by some sort of critical comment and I have not had time to do so. It is all the more difficult because this poem is not one which can be re-written: it is too good for that. No criticism of detail would matter very much. What I think is that it is too thoughtful. That is to say, the harder you think and the longer you think the better: but in turning thought into poetry it has to be fused into a more definite pattern of immediately apprehensible imagery, imagery which shall have its own validity and be immediately the equivalent of, and indeed identical with, the thought behind it.

Eliot is correct, I think, in pointing out that Blackmur had difficulty in committing his thinking to "immediately apprehensible imagery." This perhaps should not be a surprising criticism of Blackmur's poetry since committing one's thought to an image has the effect of freezing the thought much like a photograph freezes a point in time. This Blackmur was always unwilling to do and is the reason why he insisted upon the nonrigidity of words when used in poetry. When meaning can oscillate between historical uses of a word, then rigidity is avoided. This oscillation, however, is not the same thing as E. E. Cummings's use of the word "flower," to which Blackmur objected, since the oscillation is within prescribed limits and does not "float" depending entirely on particular contexts. However, the poetical problem remains the selection of "immediately apprehensible imagery." A few lines from "A Funeral for a Few Sticks" may be illustrative.

> I sit here, and this man sitting beside me,
> Both thinking, thinking a form upon the world.
> Here in this hillside place this ancient man,
> Whom I in my own might have dreamed alive,
> This man and I, and we alone, guarding
> A fire, and he feeding the flame with sticks.
> His weathered, earnest face, his earnest voice:
> Stuff of my thought. Of these I made a god.
> —But did my heart beat truly when I dreamed him?

It is no matter. I have walked with him
All day, and heard him speak, and penetrate
That secret sense which lurks beneath the skin.
I saw him stare, when he had finished talking,
Gravely across the bare brown hills, and felt
The everlasting quiet of the land
Drawn up into my veins, a numbing sap.
Then he and I were breathless images
Rooted eternally into that stillness.

I heard him speak, reduce his flesh to voice:
"If on a word I hang the sum of time,
If on a name I nail the sign of years—
All wisdom passes on my breath, and dies."
The voice snaps in the memory, a vain
Recoil. "Sweetness is only to the worm."

I made this man an oracle, to hear
The stroke of being, beat on the heart's gong;
Gave him the colour of a god, may be,
That he might make the godly seem more real,
That he might sheathe the shadow of our dream
With human flesh and human memory.
Being matured among the dead, he sprang
Among the living old, and glitters where
Old thought becomes a sense, the sense a voice.

The rest of the poem contains philosophical musings of the kind one might have sitting in front of a fire somewhere on a beach. The problem Eliot is pointing to is that the image of fire and an old man is not sufficient to carry the weight of such musings. The reader is really at a loss to understand why these thoughts have appeared here at this time and what significance they have to his life, labor, and thought. In other words, the imagery is not immediately apprehensible.

Blackmur himself gives evidence of a curious reluctance to commit himself to his poems as completed entities. More than most poets, he was always ready to accept rearrangement, new lines, and even new titles from his editors. In a letter to Harriet Monroe, the editor of *Poetry Magazine,* Blackmur wrote:[4]

I am very glad that you found it possible to accept my poems. The grouping that you suggest seems proper to me; it seems to give them a

sequence and a climax I would not have thought they possessed. —But
for the title you ask, I can do nothing. I am never able to think of titles
except the dullest, and therefore surrender the labour to others
whenever possible. If you think of anything that seems suitable please
affix it. And I, if God gives me one, will send it on. Otherwise, I suppose
they will have to be called Five poems, tout court; a kind of baptism
which never takes, and is indeed getting out of fashion.

Such diffidence comes not from insecurity or a lack of mastery,
but rather from a habit of mind that characterizes Blackmur.
"Thinking about thinking," or, "thinking about thinking about
love, sex, etc.," were, as often as not, his real themes. Since it was
the thinking process itself that was important to him, fixed titles,
apprehensible imagery, and the arrangement of lines were of
secondary importance. (This is not the same as saying "of no
importance"). The judgment here must be personal, but I offer as
an example of how Blackmur's focus could interfere with the
poetic success of his poems a work from his first volume entitled
"Simulacrum Deae."

> Having admired, and in admiring sired
> desire, the firm long line from waist to knee,
> having by accident and warmth of wine
> suddenly let my eyes go free in hers,
> I stopped, seizing within me the stilled second
> before the threatened thunderclap occurs.
>
> Slowly I turned, thunder about my ears,
> the suffering of wonder in my eyes;
> she who had been half handsome stranger, half
> casual friend, that second had become
> a face for desparate homage, and amends.
>
> I looked and she was newly flesh, her arms
> intensive, calm, and round, her likewise
> fresh with the first ease of intimacy
> burned through their own darkness to the light;
> and I began to think with lips and eyelids,
> with all the tender motions of the body,
> sharp or confused, in loin or fingertips,
> that may, guided, encouraged, firm the mind
> to meet the crisis of another's being;
> and with the greater, aching tenderness

> shaking in unspoken words, unseen seeing,
> wherein there is no purpose or disguise,
> only a blind mind discovering a blind.
>
> —How sweet the torment in this structure joins
> the hope that monuments its own despair.
> The trembling animal inside my loins
> inside my heart my head my soul rose up
> to search the inscrutable fastness of her being,
> to seize only the face that was not there.

To my mind, the poem is fully realized in the first eleven lines of the first two stanzas. The sudden recognition of desire where heretofore only friendship had been is one of those delightful occurrences that happens now and then. Enough said. But no, Blackmur needs to analyze the recognition into its constituent parts, thereby attentuating, at least for me, the effect of the poem.

Writing poetry was not easy for Blackmur. He published his first book of verse rather late (age thirty-three) in his career, an indication, I think, of the problems Eliot alludes to in his letter. In 1935, as he was readying *From Jordan's Delight* for publication, Blackmur sent the title poem to Morton Dauwen Zabel, who had taken over the editorship at *Poetry Magazine* from Harriet Monroe. Zabel rejected the poem for publication in *Poetry* and Blackmur responded in a long, illuminating letter:[5]

It is hard for me to see the poem as complicated, or as full of ambition, or as self-engrossed. I had tried to join certain projections of sea-island landscape, certain images out of my countryside, and, as they seemed in my mind, natural analogues, certain projections from the landscape of my reading and the sharp edge of affairs; and tried to do so as "objectively" as possible—by which I mean only in words that would carry their own meaning. The literary references which you find positively distressing do not seem to me literary at all, certainly far less literary than references to the Cross or to Lincoln would be; though I should not hesitate to use them on that ground. Montaigne and Baudelaire, for example, represent for me a profound and omnipresent antithesis which, as I think, *ought* to be apparent to others as soon as declared; similarly the antithesis of Shakespeare and Milton. But I see my *ought* is a mere rhetorical imperative for others at just the point where for me it flows out of envisaged landscape. My wife feels exactly as you do as to the words I have used, yet shares (as I hope you may, imaginatively) the emotional projection I intended to represent. So, with Miss Moore [Marianne Moore] I have three against me; and I confess I feel I must draw back—believing, as I must, that my responsibility is to other's readng, not my own. I shall if I can dress out my images otherwise in the poem, or at any rate try to *enforce* them as they are so that readers like the editors of Poetry and my wife may be willing to accept them as, essentially, they are. In short, I accept your objections on technical grounds, which are for me, as you know, the best of all grounds; and if I have any success in changing my modes you will see the poem again. Otherwise I shall try publication elsewhere. I sometimes think that I live mistakenly apart from others who write verse; that I might do better with more immediate inspection and argument.

Blackmur's distress must have been evident to Zabel because he immediately wrote a reply.[6]

I must still stick to my adjectives: I would still use them, admiringly, if you had succeeded. Certainly I have no objection to the use of literary references (or motivation, or complexities) in a poem; but the poem must succeed in establishing itself as their appropriate medium. When it doesn't they stand out with the kind of depressing obviousness I tried to describe. The "profound and omnipresent antithesis" which you say "*ought* to be apparent to others as soon as declared" (in Montaigne and Baudelaire) IS apparent. I had no difficulty in sighting it; I had too little. Certainly you must have "shared imaginatively the emotional projection I intended to represent" as fully as I tried (though perhaps not too articularly or successfully) to share yours in my letter (even though in letters the projection should not be emotional). What I do wish to project, and with as emotional a sincerity as I can muster, is my sympathy for your purposes as a poet, and my distress at sensing the reason why they miscarry. I hope that we don't have to agree with Goldsmith, Macauley, and Mr. Richards that a scientific and analytical intelligence diminishes the poetic faculty, but it seems almost inevitably to scatter that talent's forces and to make the certain decision of a personal poetic style—in all but a few cases—very elusive. Your equipment is so remarkable that of course it makes your poetic problem all the more painful. But honestly, your poems haven't yet hit on a style; they are too various in manner; they expose their processes and distractions instead of including and "realizing" them. That is "the thing essentially impossible" that I spoke of. I am sure you don't believe that I consider the apposition of seascape and literature absurd, given the proper circumstances and compulsion.

Blackmur's reply was full of hurt feelings and resigned

fortitude. "I will struggle on with *From Jordan's Delight,* chaotic structure and all; but I doubt you will see it again—it is already too much what I believe I want for me to cast it all in one form. I admit the disintegrative effect; but it is not so for me: it is half-united; which is enough."[7]

Allen Tate's review of *From Jordan's Delight* in the *Southern Review* was, however, generally laudatory.[8] Calling Blackmur "one of the best poets of our time," Tate praised his "high sense of form" and commented that his poetry "combines the richness of perception and the apparent abandonment to the flux of experience, usually found in the romantic poets, with high form and implicit intellectual order." Yet Tate found it necessary, as had Eliot and Zabel, to point to what he thought was the central problem confronting Blackmur as a poet.

> Blackmur writes from two different *points d'appui,* the one abstract, the other immediate and dramatic. . . . Mr. Blackmur takes the "idea" first, and tries second to reduce it to image, with the result that the images do not materialize out of the idea. Of course, a merely logical reversal of this method would not remedy the trouble; but to state it so, on the bare logical basis, is enough I think to indicate the kind of defect that renders unsound this phase of Blackmur's work. Blackmur as a critic is a master of ideas, but as a poet he is occasionally mastered by them. But this does not mean that the idea as such, as a critical analysis of the function of poetry in relation to action, is unsound; it is rather that the idea is not available to Blackmur on the level of poetry. And this limitation witnesses again the difficulty of our age in writing philosophical poetry—a poetry springing from an appreciation, however profound, of ideas.

Tate's comment on the difficulty of writing philosophical verse gives a clue, I think, to why Blackmur's criticism shifted its focus, after *The Double Agent,* to the critic's responsibility to build bridges, foster understanding, and interpret Western culture to itself. Obviously, for philosophical poetry to be appreciated, much less understood, the ideas referred to in the poetry must be ideas generally shared by the poet's society. This is a necessary precondition before a poet of ideas, as no doubt Blackmur thought himself to be, can even have a chance to be understood, much less appreciated.

It is not surprising that Blackmur found himself living "apart from others who write verse" in the twentieth century. He knew that his artistic problem was that his mode and manner did not fit either his audience or his time. In this he believed he shared a spiritual kinship with Henry Adams. Yet the fact remains that Yeats, Eliot, Thomas, Frost, Auden, and many others faced and still face the same set of circumstances and were able to write successful poetry. The solution to Blackmur's failure as a poet is, as Tate suggests, that he chose to write from the idea on back to the image—a poetic method that is successful only when the poet shares with his audience, as Dante did, a common sack of ideas, goals, pretensions, and madnesses.

Blackmur's *The Second World* was a slim volume published at the beginning of America's entry into WW II. The poems are, for the most part, less successful attempts to organize personal feelings in relation to world events. It is possible that Blackmur believed the war to be the political equivalent of the spiritual anarchy faced by all sensitive souls in the twentieth century. If so, part of that anarchy would have been for him the various ideologies and instances of doctrinaire thought, both here and abroad. As we know from his "A Critic's Job of Work" essay, Blackmur disliked and distrusted ideological or doctrinaire thought, preferring instead the ongoing process of thinking. Many of the poems in this volume refer to his observation of the human predilection to respond to war, economic deprivation, and disorder with thought rather than with thinking. "Una Vita Nuova" is a good example.

> That crazy wretch got up
> and donned sea-going clothes.
> "Tomtit," says he, "tom tup,
> how lately blooms the rose!"
> So instinct runs away.
>
> That tireless fag went out,
> the sea was spattered sun.
> "Such goodness all about
> and I am overrun."
> So instinct skims away.
>
> That hireling in arrear
> sat down to ease his legs.
> "I wear man's tiring-gear,"
> cries he, "and nothing begs."
> So instinct pours away.

That tired miser fished,
his livelong self as bait.
"I've caught before I wished
the flounder in heaven's strait."
So instinct scales away.

He turned, all flounder-faint,
in hope of human eyes.
"All beggar, all complaint,
all pierced I am," he cries:
all instinct skun away.

The best poem is the title poem, "The Second World."

Who that has sailed by star
on the light night-air,
first hand on the tiller,
second, the nibbling sheet,

who, looking aloft and then aback,
has not one moment lost
in the wind's still eye
his second world
and the bright star

before the long shudder fills on
the windward tack?

Here Blackmur makes a successful connection between loss of
control, disorder, anarchy and that momentary loss of helm and
sail control when changing tacks on a sailboat. Once again,
Blackmur is at his best in short poems with imagery related to
the sea.

The most successful poems in Blackmur's last volume of verse,
The Good European, again were those that were short and
compressed. "The Skin of the Soul," part ii of "Twelve Scarabs
for the Living: 1942," is particularly effective.

If righteousness without its faith is sin
and faith without its sin is empty act,
how shall the armed man plead? or soul save skin?
Between the lover and his murder pact
there is the third lost face, self looking in.

The critical reaction to *The Good European* was mixed. John Malcolm Brinnin praised "Twelve Scarabs," stating that from them "comes a conviction that the ideas and feelings expressed have come a long way, through many revisions of language and carefully tooled phrasing, to the exact point of abstraction which allows them universality without loss of sensory warmth or emotional flexibility."[9] Harold Norse, on the other hand, thought that "in some insidious way, death has permeated too deeply into the subconscious of this poet, and has killed off, or numbed, the first person singular. It is easier for him to talk about the universal situation particularized, than the personal situation universalized."[10]

Brinnin and Norse, with Eliot, Zabel, and Tate, point to the essential character of Blackmur's poetry. It is carefully crafted but without life. When the poetry is read against the background of late-nineteenth- and early twentieth-century poetry, one can observe how conservative Blackmur was in his use of poetic strategies. In his criticism as well as in his poetry, Blackmur distrusted modernist thought and procedure as assaults on the intellect. The "techniques of trouble" concept extended also to poetic techniques and strategies. This idea, however, seems to have severely limited his poetic resources. While one may detect echoes of Yeats, Eliot, Hopkins, Stevens, and Crane, Blackmur could not emulate their success. Ultimately, he could not discover a style that was his and which did not, in his own mind, contribute to the "great grasp of unreason." But Blackmur would not compromise by adopting an aesthetic form at the expense of reason. Therein lies his own scrupulosity, the characteristic he admired so much in Henry Adams—a scrupulosity Blackmur called "the expense of greatness."

CHAPTER 8

Blackmur in Perspective

I Aristotle and Coleridge

IT may be said that Blackmur started his career in the ideological climate of the eighteenth century and ended it in
that of the nineteenth. In other words, he began as a Classicist
with Romantic elements in his criticism and ended as a
Romanticist with Classic elements. Since Blackmur himself was
not a systematic theorist it is difficult to be precise about any
theory he might have had, but I believe that the poetic theory
distilled from his essays on various poets illustrates the eighteenth-century Classicism in his critical thought while his essays
on the critic's job and on literature and Henry Adams illustrate
the progressively Romantic orientation he took as his career
progressed.

The theory of poetic creation described in Chapter 2 parallels
those that may be found at the height of neo-classicism in the
eighteenth century. The eighteenth-century literary theorists
adopted a mechanical description of the creative process in the
hope of emulating the work of physical scientists in the field of
mechanics. They felt that the method used by the scientists to
solve problems in or of Nature could also be applied to problems
of creativity. From their application of scientific method to the
problems of creativity came a mechanistic theory of literary
invention. They likened the mind to a machine which "pro-
cessed" the raw material of sense experience into the completed
work of art. Creativity in their theories was described as the
putting together of parts or the breaking down of wholes into
their constituent parts. The mind, they said, received sense data
and either broke it down into its constituent parts or associated
the parts of sense experience into regular and homogeneous
aggregations. The mind performed this wonderful operation by
the turning of the "gears" of imagination and reason. These two

152

faculties of the mind operated almost exactly as they were described as acting in Blackmur's theory of poetic creativity. The imagination seized "the individual from the flux," and it qualified, evaluated, and reintensified the sense data. Reason patterned, controlled, and ordered what imagination selected.

There is another characteristic of Blackmur's poetic theory that gives it a Classic flavor. In any mechanistic description of the creative process there arises the problem of artistic design and critical judgment. If, in the eighteenth-century view (which Blackmur shares), the mind is a machine that simply "acts" or "works" on the sense experience it receives from the outside world, then how is it that the incoherent pattern of sense experience becomes ordered into an artistic design? That is, how do reason and imagination "know" what pattern or design they want for the work of art? To answer this question the eighteenth-century literary theorists introduced the concept of the intelligent "ghost in the machine" that devises a blue-print or plan that reason and imagination follow. This plan was thought of as a unity, or as an inherent teleological design by which the artist's mind focused and ordered his sense experience. In Blackmur's poetic theory, this teleological design became the artist's "view of life." Eliot had his religion, Yeats had his magic, and Blackmur himself had his fusion of Numen and Moha. All sense experience was for him made meaningful in terms of this design.

There are other elements of Blackmur's poetic theory that are Classic—such as his emphasis on the medium of poetry. In the early stages of his career, Blackmur's emphasis on language seemed to put him in the New Critical camp. As I mentioned in Chapter 1 the New Critics sought *objectively* to evaluate poetry by analyzing its structure. In other words they sought to evaluate the content by evaluating the form. Blackmur seems never to have wanted to go quite that far. He did indeed use language as a standard for critical evaluation of poems, yet he seems to have relied more upon notions of taste and sensibility to evaluate poetic language than upon the New Critical criteria of irony and paradox. He would have agreed thoroughly with Alexander Pope that poetic language should combine sound with sense and express what often was thought but never so well expressed.

There are also Romantic elements in Blackmur's poetic theory. One of these is his view of the poem as part of a social nexus linking the poet to his society. To Blackmur the poem reflected the mental activity of the poet and it also reflected the springs and motives of his psychology. The relationship of the poem to the psychology of the poet was a Romantic emphasis and one Blackmur also chose to emphasize because it gave his criticism wider scope. Considerations of the poet's psychology allowed him to bring social considerations under review because he believed that society conditioned the poet. It is this particular emphasis in Blackmur's criticism that is developed and exploited in his later career and which gives to his later criticism the theoretical justification for its impressionistic form.

Another Romantic element in Blackmur's poetic theory involves an apparent contradiction. If he allowed that poetry expresses the poet's psychology, then why did he get so upset over E. E. Cummings? Almost all of Cummings's poems have their source in his feelings; I have already noted Blackmur's objection that no one can ever express his feelings directly. Was Blackmur really objecting to the expressive (Romantic) theory of poetic creation when he objected to Cummings's and to D. H. Lawrence's poetry? In part he was, insofar as he understood that the Romantics expressed themselves *directly*. If they did, he thought, then there was no room for reason. But the fact remains that Blackmur allowed that interior states of mind could legitimately be the subject matter of poetry. Wallace Stevens, as Romantic a poet as Cummings, was one of Blackmur's favorites. It seems, then, that Blackmur allowed Romantic subject matter like the feelings and moods of the poet without allowing the poet the Romantic methodology for expressing them. In this he was following some Romantic theorists like Hazlitt who espoused the doctrine that the expression of personal moods and feelings must be in forms concrete and particularized so that they may be understood. Otherwise poetry would degenerate into mere egoism. Blackmur's poetic theory, then, has a Classicist's description of the creative process combined with a Romantic's conception of the nature of poetry.

The criticism Blackmur wrote in his later years is more Romantic in style and theoretical in orientation than Classic. As I pointed out in the last chapter, his style in his Library of Congress essays and other later works was to use language more expressively than cognitively. That his theoretical orientation was more Romantic can be seen chiefly in his insistence that art expresses culture—indeed, that art is an organic expression of culture. Blackmur constantly emphasized the growing, changing nature of art. That was why the act of criticism as he called it had to be done over and over again. Art and artists were constantly growing and shifting in relation to themselves and to culture. To say this another way, Richard Palmer Blackmur was a Romantic because his fundamental insight was that all art, artists, societies, cultures, and social forms were part of a complex interrelation of living, indeterminate, and endlessly changing components. But because he perceived that this complex, interrelated culture was coming apart, he stressed the reason's order-creating capacity, and this stress tempered his Romanticism.

II *Literary Contribution and the Permanent Value*

Blackmur's contribution to literature may be found in the form of the critical essays he wrote during the later phases of his career. The Library of Congress essays, in particular, represent the form of the critical essay that marks his unique contribution. These essays were his attempt to raise criticism to a new plane of discourse.

Briefly put, Blackmur attempted to incorporate into these essays an expression of his aesthetic experience of literature and of culture. Thus, in effect, he tried to "open" the form of the critical essay by giving equal emphasis to the nonrational expression of his own experience. Prior to Blackmur's practice, critical essayists had always tried to be, with more or less success, proponents of rational thinking. Blackmur, however, made the irrational, the emotional, part of the critical essay.

His methodology for incorporating the irrational was borrowed from the poets and novelists of the late nineteenth and early twentieth centuries. It consisted chiefly of the device of analogical form, whereby the creative artist or critic chose some image or symbol to express an interior state of feeling. As described in Chapter 6, analogical form makes it possible for artists to express their feelings of disorder, alienation, and isolation by putting disparate images of each together in the same work.

Blackmur extended the use of analogical form to include concepts linked together in such a way that together they would create an effect and simultaneously be an expression of feeling. To illustrate, let us take the phrase "techniques of trouble" introduced in Chapter 6. The two linked concepts are embodied in the terms "techniques" and "trouble." "Techniques" refers to what Blackmur calls the "new knowledges" of psychology, anthropology, sociology, and psychiatry. "Trouble" refers to Blackmur's belief that these "new knowledges" have undermined the complete self by fragmenting it into separate and distinct parts and creating, in the process, an almost undecipherable jargon.

By putting these two terms together, Blackmur created a poetic rendering of his own experience of twentieth-century culture. "Techniques of trouble" is not a term meant to be understood by reason alone. On the contrary, in using the term and others like it, Blackmur hoped to engender in his reader an aesthetic appreciation that augmented and amplified the intellectual understanding of his essays.

I should point out immediately here that Blackmur did not mean to discount the rational understanding of his essays. Rather, he sought what he thought should be a *total* experience that included the irrational with the rational. In this desire he was seeking for the art of criticism what modern artists had sought for painting, poetry, the novel, and music. Blackmur did not want his criticism to point to an experience but to *be* an experience. In this way he extended the scope and the form of literary criticism.

In addition to raising criticism to the level of a legitimate art form, Blackmur also contributed a whole body of work that will have permanent value as long as there is a Western culture. Throughout his work Blackmur questioned the lack of standards to judge not only art but life, liberty, and the pursuit of happiness. He was against the democratic inclusiveness of the spirit that meant whatever is done must perforce be "creative." At the same time he agonized over the question of creativity and its manifestations in a democratic, romantic age. In his own work he applied the scrupulosity he admired so much in Henry Adams; that is, he took pains to give his essays a "form" as well as a content. Put another way, Blackmur thought he could control unbridled romantic effusions of spirit by insisting upon a rigorous attention to form.

All of his work has a certain tension that derives from this conflict between form and content, reason and imagination. Blackmur fought the same battle that every twentieth-century artist has fought and must fight. His particular art form was criticism, but it could have been poetry or the novel. In the last analysis, his work must be seen as his unique attempt to create order and meaning out of the undifferentiated chaos of the spirit. So Blackmur becomes one with the many who have built their own edifices of meaning through art.

Notes and References

Chapter One

1. Alfred Alvarez, "R. P. Blackmur (1904-1965)," *Review: A Magazine of Poetry and Criticism* 18(1968): 21.
2. Letter, Allen Tate to Blackmur, April 4, 1937: Blackmur Collection, Princeton.
3. Letter, Richard Eberhart to Blackmur, March (no date), 1938: Blackmur Collection, Princeton.
4. Letter, T. S. Eliot to Blackmur, July 30, 1926: Blackmur Collection, Princeton.
5. John Crowe Ransom, "Criticism as Pure Speculation," *The Intent of the Critic*, ed. Donald A. Stauffer (New York: Bantam, 1966), p. 86.
6. Murray Krieger, *The New Apologists for Poetry* (Minneapolis: University of Minnesota, 1956), 147.
7. "The Lion and the Honeycomb," *The Lion and the Honeycomb* (New York: Harcourt, 1955), p. 190.
8. Ibid.
9. "Notes on E. E. Cummings' Poetry," *The Double Agent* (Gloucester, Mass.: Peter Smith, 1962), p. 2.
10. "A Critic's Job of Work," *The Double Agent*, p. 299.
11. "The Enabling Act of Criticism," *American Issues*, ed. Willard Thorp (Philadelphia: Lippincott, 1941), p. 879.
12. "The Jew in Search of a Son: Joyce's Ulysses," *Eleven Essays in the European Novel* (New York: Harcourt, 1964), p. 27.
13. "The Critical Prefaces of Henry James," *The Double Agent*, p. 267.

Chapter Two

1. "T. S. Eliot: II," *Hound and Horn* I(1928): 304.
2. Ibid., p. 303.
3. "The Great Grasp of Unreason," *A Primer of Ignorance*, ed. Joseph Frank (New York: Harcourt, 1967), p. 4.
4. "Notes on Four Categories in Criticism," *The Lion and the Honeycomb*, p. 218.
5. "Notes on the Criticism of Herbert Read," *Larus* I(1928): 52.
6. "T. S. Eliot: II," p. 313.
7. "Notes on the Criticism of Herbert Read," p. 52.

8. "Notes on E. E. Cummings' Language," *The Double Agent*, p. 28.

9. "D. H. Lawrence and Expressive Form," *The Double Agent*, p. 114.

10. "In The Hope of Straightening Things Out," *The Lion and the Honeycomb*, p. 172.

11. "Notes on E. E. Cummings' Language," p. 13.

12. "T. S. Eliot: II," p. 313.

13. "D. H. Lawrence and Expressive Form," p. 107.

14. "T. S. Eliot: I," *Hound and Horn* I(1928): 187.

15. "T. S. Eliot: II," p. 315.

16. "D. H. Lawrence and Expressive Form," p. 114.

17. "Notes on E. E. Cummings' Language," pp. 8-9.

18. Ibid., p. 9.

19. Ibid., p. 10.

20. "Examples of Wallace Stevens," *The Double Agent*, p. 71.

21. Ibid., p. 72.

22. Ibid., p. 75.

23. "Notes on E. E. Cummings' Language," p. 13.

24. "Notes on the Criticism of Herbert Read," p. 55.

25. "T. S. Eliot: II," p. 296.

26. Ibid.

27. "Notes on E. E. Cummings' Language," p. 10.

28. Ibid., p. 12.

29. "T. S. Eliot: II," p. 305.

30. "D. H. Lawrence and Expressive Form," p. 104.

31. "New Thresholds, New Anatomies. Notes on a Text of Hart Crane," *The Double Agent*, pp. 121-40.

32. "Examples of Wallace Stevens," *The Double Agent*, p. 94.

33. "The Later Poetry of W. B. Yeats," *The Expense of Greatness* (Gloucester, Mass.: Peter Smith, 1958), pp. 74-75.

34. "T. S. Eliot. From Ash Wednesday to Murder in the Cathedral," *The Double Agent*, p. 187.

35. "The Later Poetry of W. B. Yeats," p. 77.

Chapter Three

1. "A Critic's Job of Work," *The Double Agent*, pp. 269-302.

2. "The Enabling Act of Criticism," *American Issues*, p. 879.

3. "Language as Gesture," *Accent* III(1942): 30-44.

4. "A Burden for Critics," *The Lion and the Honeycomb*, p. 199.

5. "The Lion and the Honeycomb," *The Lion and the Honeycomb*, p. 184.

6. "A Featherbed for Critics," *The Expense of Greatness*, pp. 277-305.

7. "The Lion and the Honeycomb," pp. 176-97.

Chapter Four

1. Henry Adams, *The Education of Henry Adams*, p. 475.
2. Ibid.
3. Ibid., p. 484.
4. Ibid., p. 485.
5. Ibid., p. 487.
6. "The Expense of Greatness," in *The Expense of Greatness*, p. 253.
7. "Adams Goes to School: 1. The Problem Laid Out." *Kenyon Review* 18(1955): 597-99.
8. Ibid., p. 600.
9. "The Expense of Greatness," pp. 273-74.
10. "Adams Goes to School," p. 604.
11. "The Novels of Henry Adams," *A Primer of Ignorance*, p. 203.
12. Ibid., p. 202.
13. Ibid., p. 214.
14. Ibid., p. 215.
15. Ibid., p.220.
16. Ibid., p. 216.
17. Ibid., pp. 224-25.
18. Ibid., pp. 201-202.
19. "The Expense of Greatness," p. 267.
20. "Adams Goes to School," p. 605.
21. Ibid., p. 602.
22. "The Expense of Greatness," p. 271.
23. "Adams Goes to School," p. 603.

Chapter Five

1. "The Brothers Karamazov: I, "*Eleven Essays in the European Novel* (New York: Harcourt, 1964), p. 193.
2. "The Lion and the Honeycomb," p. 293.
3. Ibid., p. 294.
4. Ibid., p. 305.
5. "The Magic Mountain," *Eleven Essays in the European Novel*, p. 76.
6. "*Ulysses,*" *Eleven Essays in the European Novel*, p. 29. The quotations in the rest of Chapter 5 can be found in the individual chapters in *Eleven Essays* denoted by the subheadings.

Chapter Six

1. "Anni-Mirabiles, 1921-1925: Reason in the Madness of Letters," *A Primer of Ignorance*, pp. 3-80. Originally published by The Library

of Congress (Washington, D.C., 1956). Hereafter cited by reference to
the individual essays that comprise *Anni-Mirabiles:* "The Great Grasp
of Unreason," "The Techniques of Trouble," "Irregular Metaphysics,"
and "Contemplation."

2. Arnold Toynbee, *A Study of History,* III, 241: quoted in "The
Great Grasp of Unreason," p. 18.

3. "The Great Grasp of Unreason," p. 18.

4. Ibid., pp. 14–15.

5. Ibid., p. 11.

6. Ibid., p. 13.

7. Ibid., p. 16.

8. "The Techniques of Trouble," p. 23. Blackmur gives his source as
Marcel Raymond's *From Baudelaire to Surrealism,* p. 270.

9. "The Techniques of Trouble," p. 24.

10. Ibid.

11. Ibid., p. 25.

12. Ibid., p. 26.

13. Ibid., p. 27.

14. Ibid., p. 28.

15. Ibid.

16. Ibid., p. 29.

17. Ibid., p. 28.

18. Ibid., p. 29.

19. Ibid., p. 30.

20. Ibid., pp. 30–31.

21. Ibid., p. 31.

22. Ibid., pp. 34–35.

23. Ibid., p. 36.

24. "The Great Grasp of Unreason," p. 8.

25. Ibid., pp. 8–9.

26. Ibid., pp. 9–10.

27. "Irregular Metaphysics," p. 38.

28. Ibid., p. 40.

29. Ibid., p. 41.

30. Ibid., pp. 41–42.

31. Ibid., p. 42.

32. Ibid.

33. Ibid., pp. 43–44.

34. Ibid., p. 44.

35. Ibid., pp. 44–45.

36. Ibid., p. 46.

37. Ibid., p. 53.

38. Ibid., p. 58.

Chapter Seven

1. *Poems of R. P. Blackmur,* intro. Denis Donoghue (Princeton, N.J.: Princeton University Press, 1977). p. 8. Poems are cited from this edition.

2. "Notes on E. E. Cummings' Language," *The Double Agent,* p. 8.

3. Letter, T. S. Eliot to Blackmur, July 30, 1926: Blackmur Collection, Princeton.

4. Letter, Blackmur to Harriet Monroe, January 22, 1933: *Poetry Magazine* Collection, University of Chicago Library.

5. Letter, Blackmur to Zabel, November 12, 1935: *Poetry Magazine* Collection.

6. Letter, Zabel to Blackmur, November 14, 1935: *Poetry Magazine* Collection.

7. Letter, Blackmur to Zabel, February 10, 1936: *Poetry Magazine* Collection.

8. Allen Tate, "R. P. Blackmur and Others," *Southern Review* III(1937): 196.

9. John Malcolm Brinnin, "To Be or Not: 5 Opinions on R. P. Blackmur's *The Good European,*" *Tiger's Eye,* 3, 67. (listed in the Index to Little Magazines).

10. Harold Norse, Ibid., p. 72.

Selected Bibliography

PRIMARY SOURCES

1. Books of Criticism

The Double Agent: Essays in Craft and Elucidation. New York: Arrow Editions, 1935. Reprinted: Gloucester, Mass.: Peter Smith, 1962.

The Expense of Greatness. New York: Arrow Editions, 1940. Reprinted: Gloucester, Mass.: Peter Smith, 1958.

Language As Gesture: Essays in Poetry. New York: Harcourt, Brace and Company, 1952.

Form and Value in Modern Poetry. New York: Doubleday, 1952.

The Lion and the Honeycomb: Essays in Solicitude and Critique. New York: Harcourt, Brace and Company, 1955.

Anni Mirabiles 1921-1925: Reason in the Madness of Letters. Washington, D.C.: Library of Congress, 1956.

New Criticism in the United States. Tokyo: Kenkyusha Press, 1959.

Eleven Essays in the European Novel. New York: Harcourt, Brace and Company, 1964.

A Primer of Ignorance. Edited by Joseph Frank. New York: Harcourt, Brace and World, 1967.

2. Books of Poetry

From Jordan's Delight. Arrow Editions: New York, 1937.

The Second World. Cummington, Mass.: The Cummington Press, 1942.

The Good European And Other Poems. Cummington, Mass.: The Cummington Press, 1947.

Poems of R. P. Blackmur. Princeton, N.J.: Princeton University Press, 1977.

3. Introductions

JAMES, HENRY. *The Art of the Novel.* New York: Scribner's, 1934.

WHEELWRIGHT, JOHN. *Selected Poems.* Norfolk: New Directions Press, 1941.

JAMES, HENRY. *The Golden Bowl.* New York: Dell, 1952.

———. *Washington Square.* New York: Dell, 1959.

———. *The American.* New York: Dell, 1960.

———. *American Short Novels.* New York: T. Y. Crowell, 1960.

AIKEN, CONRAD. *Collected Novels of Conrad Aiken.* New York: Holt, Rinehart and Winston, 1964.

4. Pamphlets
For Any Book. Cambridge, Mass.: Privately printed by F. W. Murray and Rowe, 1924.
A Funeral for a Few Sticks. Lynn, Mass.: Lone Gull Press, 1927.
T. S. Eliot. Cambridge, Mass.: Hound and Horn, 1928.
Dirty Hands or The True Born Censor. Cambridge, England: Minority Press, 1930. Pseud. Perry Hobbs.
Psyche in the South. Tryon, N.C.: Tryon Pamphlets, 1934.

SECONDARY SOURCES

1. Bibliographies
BAKER, CARLOS. "R. P. Blackmur: A Checklist," *Princeton University Library Chronicle* 3 (April 1942): 99–106.
PANNICK, GERALD J. *Richard Palmer Blackmur: A Bibliography, Bulletin of Bibliography* 31(Oct.–Dec.), 1974.
TATE, ALLEN. *Sixty American Poets 1896–1944.* Washington, D.C.: Library of Congress, 1954.

2. General Criticism
CREWS, FREDERICK C. *The Pooh Perplex.* New York: E. P. Dutton, 1963. Parody of Blackmur's style and critical vision in chapter by "P. R. Honeycomb."
DONOGHUE, DENIS. "Poetic in the Common Enterprise," *Twentieth Century* 161(June 1957): 537–46. Discusses Blackmur's work in terms of Kenneth Burke's pentad of Act, Scene, Agent, Agency, and Purpose.
FOSTER, RICHARD. "R. P. Blackmur: The Technical Critic as Romantic Agonist," Western Review 23(1959): 259–70. Seeks to reassess Blackmur's reputation as a technical critic in the light of the evidence of his statements about such nontechnical concerns as "life-force" and "theoretic form of the soul."
FRANK, JOSEPH. "R. P. Blackmur: The Later Phase," *The Widening Gyre.* New Brunswick, N.J.: Rutgers University Press, 1963. Sympathetic reading of Blackmur's critical purposes and strategies in his later essays.
HYMAN, STANLEY EDGAR. "R. P. Blackmur and the Expense of Criticism," *Poetry* 71(1948): 259–70. Reprinted in Hyman's *The Armed Vision.* Emphasizes Blackmur's concern for the structure of poetry and his intellectual fastidiousness.
KAZIN, ALFRED. "Criticism and Isolation," *Virginia Quarterly Review* 17(1942): 448–53. Questions whether Blackmur is more interested in criticism for its own sake than in literature.
LEWIS, R. W. B. "Casella as Critic: A Note on R. P. Blackmur." *Kenyon Review* 13(1951): 458–74. An excellent essay on Blackmur's critical style and ideas.

PRITCHARD, WILLIAM H. "R. P. Blackmur and the Criticism of Poetry," *Massachusetts Review* 8(1967): 633-49. An overview of Blackmur's major critical insights in forty years of poetry criticism.

SCHWARTZ, DELMORE. "The Critical Method of R. P. Blackmur," *Poetry* 53(1938): 28-29. Excellent critique of Blackmur's early criticism.

WEST, RAY B., JR. "R. P. Blackmur," *Rocky Mountain Review* 8(1944): 139-45. Relates Blackmur's critical method to T. S. Eliot's.

Index